FRANCISCAN STUDIES

VOL. XX

THE FRANCISCANS IN MEDIEVAL ENGLISH LIFE (1224-1348)

FRANCISCAN STUDIES

A series of monographs dealing with subjects of Franciscan history and Franciscan science, published at irregular intervals under the auspices of the Franciscan, Conventual and Capuchin Fathers of the English-speaking countries of the world.

The following is a complete list of titles thus far published:

1. *Science in the Franciscan Order: A Historical Sketch.* By John M. Lenhart, O. M. Cap. .... $ .25
2. *St. Bonaventure: The Seraphic Doctor.* By Ludger Wegemer, O. F. M., and Vincent Mayer, O. M. Conv. .... .25
3. *The Origin and Development of the Franciscan School; Duns Scotus.* By Berard Vogt, O. F. M. (out of print) .... .25
4. *Ven. John Duns Scotus: Life, Works, Doctrine.* By Edwin Dorzweiler, O. M. Cap., Raphael M. Huber, O. M. Conv., Vincent Mayer, O. M. Conv. (out of print) .... .25

5. *Language Studies in the Franciscan Order: A Historical Sketch.* By John M. Lenhart, O. M. Cap. (out of print) .... $ .75

6. *Franciscan Mysticism: The Mystical Theology of the Seraphic Doctor.* By Dunstan Dobbins, O. M. Cap 1.25

7. *History of Franciscan Preaching and of Franciscan Preachers* (*1209-1927*). By Anscar Zawart, O. M. Cap. 1.50

8. *The Capuchins in French Louisiana* (*1722-1766*). By Claude L. Vogel, O. M. Cap. (out of print) 1.50

9. *Père Girard, Educator.* By Andrew Maas, O. M. Conv. .... .50

10. *Ignatius Cardinal Persico, O. M. Cap.* By Donald Shearer, O. M. Cap.; *Pioneer Capuchin Missionaries in the United States* (*1784-1816*). By Norbert Miller, O. M. Cap. .... .75

11. *Pontificia Americana: A Documentary History of the Catholic Church in the United States* (*1784-1884*). By Donald Shearer, O. M. Cap. ... 1.25

12. *The Ludwig-Missionsverein and the Church in the United States* (*1838-1918*). By Theodore Roemer, O. M. Cap. .... .75

13. *The Franciscan Père Marquette: Father Zénobe Membré, O. F. M.* By Marion Habig, O. F. M. 1.25

14. *Pre-Reformation Printed Books.* By John M. Lenhart, O. M. Cap. 1.00

15. *Catholic Leadership toward Social Progress: The Third Order.* By Marion Habig, O. F. M. (out of print) .... .50

16. *Pioneer Capuchin Letters.* By Theodore Roemer, O. M. Cap. 1.00

17. *Roger Bacon's Contribution to Knowledge.* By Edward Lutz, O. F. M. ... .50

18. *The Martyrs of Florida* (*1513-1616*), *by Luis Geronimo de Oré.* Translated by Maynard Geiger, O. F. M. 1.00

19. *The Portiuncula Indulgence from Honorius III to Pius XI.* By Raphael M. Huber, O. M. Conv. ....paper 1.25
cloth 2.00

20. *The Franciscans in Medieval English Life* (*1224-1348*). By Victor G. Green, O. M. Cap. .... paper 1.50
cloth 2.00

FRANCISCAN STUDIES

VOL. XX

THE FRANCISCANS IN MEDIEVAL ENGLISH LIFE

(1224-1348)

By

VICTOR G. GREEN, O. M. CAP., B. LITT. (OXON.)

ST. ANTHONY GUILD PRESS
PATERSON, N. J.
1939

Imprimi potest.
Fr. Ignatius Weisbruch, O. M. Cap.,
Minister Provincialis.

Pittsburgh, Dec. 3, 1938.

Nihil obstat.
Arthur J. Scanlan, S. T. D.,
Censor Librorum.

Imprimatur.
✠ Stephen J. Donahue, D. D.,
Administrator, New York.

New York, March 25, 1939.

PRINTED IN THE UNITED STATES OF AMERICA

EDITOR'S PREFACE

Like the preceding number of this series,[1] the present volume is a very valuable contribution to early Franciscan history, the result of painstaking researches carried on in Europe; it is also the second work of this series which has been prepared by a student friar at Oxford University.[2]

Among other things the present work disproves, without directly intending to do so, the sweeping generalizations regarding the rapid decline of the medieval Franciscans which are sometimes found in otherwise scholarly books on the Middle Ages. In many of our colleges and universities instructors in medieval history dispose of the Franciscans in such a manner that certain students are taken aback when they learn that the Franciscans still exist at the present day. "Oh, I thought," they will tell you, "the Franciscans flourished for a few decades in the early thirteenth century and then gradually died out."

A certain university professor, who is regarded as an outstanding medievalist in the United States, and who expressed to the writer his unfeigned admiration of the civilization of the Middle Ages, observes in one of his books: "It is true that in time — and that rapidly — the Franciscans, too, declined and went the way of decrepitude and corruption like the preceding orders.... They carried in their bosom the seeds of their own ultimate failure.... The friars' scorn of property and proprietary attachments soon became a hypocritical attitude, and the friars became whining sycophants and artful beggars, employing questionable

---

1. Raphael M. Huber, *The Portiuncula Indulgence from Honorius III to Pius XI* (FRANCISCAN STUDIES, XIX). St. Anthony Guild Press, Paterson, N. J., 1938.

2. The other work is Dunstan Dobbins, *Franciscan Mysticism, a Critical Examination of the Mystical Theology of the Seraphic Doctor* (FRANCISCAN STUDIES, VI). St. Anthony Guild Press, Paterson, N. J., 1927.

methods for the extortion of funds, and rapidly delivered themselves over to avarice. As legacy hunters and hawkers of indulgences they became notorious." Perhaps this summary verdict is due to a pet formula into which the professor seems to fit the history of all religious orders: a noble beginning, a period of fervor, and a rapid or gradual decline. It is easy enough to accept without question the charges of contemporary enemies of the friars or to condemn all the Franciscans because of the unworthy or less worthy conduct of some; but the conclusions obtained after careful and detailed research, such as are offered in the present work, are unquestionably more deserving of a hearing than the broad statements in a general history.

Though it is readily conceded that the conditions which prevailed among the earliest followers of St. Francis could not possibly have been kept up as the order became a worldwide organization, the Friars Minor are frequently represented as becoming unfaithful to the ideals of St. Francis. The essential Franciscan ideal was never generally abandoned by them; as a body the Franciscans never became "hypocrites" or "delivered themselves over to avarice." Yes, abuses did creep into the order especially after the Black Death, and they were found among the Franciscans, as among others, at the time of the Protestant Revolution; but they were by no means as general as many writers would have us believe. A non-Catholic historian writes: "Luther's most earnest remonstrances were directed not against bad but against good works and the stress laid upon them by the advocates of the old religion. If that religion had been in its practice so generally corrupt as it is represented to have been by modern writers, such denunciations were idle."

Nor is it true that it was the "new orders" only which made the Catholic Reformation a success (another common error in the textbooks); the old order of the Franciscans combated the so-called reformers as much as did the new foundations, and in the Council of Trent a surprisingly large number of Franciscan theologians played a very important rôle. Far from carrying "in their bosom the seeds of their own ultimate failure," the Franciscans possess in the ideal bequeathed to them by their founder the germ of constant renewal; it blossoms forth again and again in Franciscan history, more so than in any other similar history. Down to the present day the sons of St. Francis have clung to their ideal, and have sought to conform their lives to it in as far as that is possible for human nature assisted by divine grace.

Not only to the student of history, however, is the present work one of great interest; it is also a very timely study inasmuch as it helps to clarify the true nature and worth of the medieval Franciscan message — a message which is no less valuable for the modern world. It has been said that the world of today needs another St. Francis of Assisi; but it will be of no avail merely to acknowledge the existence of such a need. Why not accept the message of the Little Poor Man — the unadulterated message in its entirety? St. Francis is living still in the great army of avowed and vested followers, several million strong, scattered over the entire globe. It is their task to exemplify, as well as to proclaim to the modern world, the saving message of the great social reformer of the thirteenth century.

In a sense every Franciscan, employing radical methods of self-reform and possessing no property of his own, is a "radical" and a "communist"; but he is the very antithesis of the modern radical and communist. While the latter wants to reform the other fellow and rob him of his property, the Franciscan aims at reforming himself and voluntarily gives up any property that might rightfully be his. He is convinced that society will be reformed only if the individual members of society of their own accord strive to better themselves, and this along the lines indicated by common sense, the commandments of God and the counsels of the Redeemer of the human race. That in a nutshell is the Franciscan message to the world; and this principle is embodied in the rule and spirit, not only of the Friars Minor and the Poor

Clares and the Third Order Regular, but also of the Third Order Secular whose members live in the family circle and move in the midst of the affairs of the world.

The Franciscan is thus unalterably opposed to totalitarianism, whether it be in the form of Communism or of Nazism. In accordance with the spirit of St. Francis, however, he distinguishes between the "ism" and the "ists." While hating the former, he is filled with genuine sympathy for the latter, whom he would like to convince that they have been duped and that their system will benefit neither themselves nor their fellow-men. In place of such crazy "isms" the Franciscan offers a simple plan of reform, which has already proved successful, has been tested by time, and will work wonders also in our modern age if it is only given a fair trial.

MARION HABIG, O. F. M.

CONTENTS

INTRODUCTION

The stress of social and economic problems in our complex modern society is responsible for many a half-wistful glance backward at the far simpler economy of the Middle Ages. We can never return to those days; few would actually care to do so. Yet somehow Christian men refuse to believe that an age which produced a St. Francis of Assisi is an age of merely historical interest. Fundamentally, man's problems are always and everywhere the same in spite of accidental differences. Hence the impetus given to the study of St. Francis by Paul Sabatier's scholarly research has developed into a new emphasis upon the Saint's claim to our attention as a social reformer. Many and various have been the claims put forth for the lessons which might be learned from medieval institutions in general and the Franciscan movement in particular. No attempt has been made in this essay to discuss or appraise these claims, but they are mentioned here as a kind of background and inspiration for the research of which the essay is a result.

From the very beginning of the investigation, however, it became evident that only disappointment awaited the student who approached the English Franciscan movement from the point of view of a social reform, in the narrow sense in which that term is generally used in our secularized society of today. As R. H. Tawney points out in *Religion and the Rise of Capitalism,* the medieval mind knew nothing of our more or less rigid division of social relations suggested by such terms as sociology, economics, politics, ethics, and the rest. The medieval hierarchical organization of society reflected a hierarchy of values also, of which the apex was religion. And this religion, with its common creed, worship and code of ethics for all, was a unifying and living principle which fused and influenced all departments of life. However much men might violate or fall short of the law and ideals set forth by this religion, they did not repudiate them. Men had not yet learned to make fine distinctions between what was morally right and what was economically expedient, and to justify their evil conduct on the basis of such a distinction.

If injustice existed, it was not blamed on the social system or the principles which were supposed to govern society, but on the misuse of the system and the failure to live up to the principles, the result of a cooling off of the religious spirit. *Revive this spirit, and evils in the system will correct themselves; justice and charity will flourish, greed and passion will be curbed; and men, by seeking the kingdom of God and His justice, will have all earthly requirements added unto them.* This, simply stated, was the essence of the Franciscan social reform. It recognized man's material and social needs, but gave them a place in its scale of values below his spiritual needs. To drive home this important principle, the Franciscans themselves gave up all ownership. To have railed against economic and social inequalities and clamored for far-reaching changes in the economic and social system without a change of heart among the individuals who made up and directed that system, would only have given earthly goods an undeserved place in the scale of values and deluded people with false hopes. Furthermore, it would have promoted class struggle, which has no place in a Christian brotherhood of men.

Hence the friars' message was predominantly spiritual, a message of revived Christianity applied to the souls of individuals. It was a harking back to Christ, who came not to abolish the law but to fulfil it, not to attack the existing order but to captivate and change the hearts of men.

These facts will help to explain why this is not a social study in the strict sense, but rather an attempt to re-create a picture, imperfect though it be, of the medieval Franciscan against the background of medieval English life. The difficulties of the task are many, some of them fairly obvious. The obscurity of the background itself, the scattered and fragmentary nature of the records, the often contradictory contemporary appraisals of the friars and their work, are some of the obstacles to a clear-cut picture.

In the selection and arrangement of materials, the writer has been guided not so much by the idea of a complete record of the friars and their activities as by the desire of presenting a true appraisal of their place and worth in the society of which they formed a part. The period covered is, roughly, the period of their heyday, from their arrival in 1224 until the Black Death in 1348. How far the Black Death was responsible for the decline of the Franciscans is a question that lies beyond the scope of this work. Dr. Holzapfel (*Handbuch der Geschichte des Franziskanerordens,* Freiburg, 1909, p. 82) agrees with Luke Wadding (*Annales Minorum,* VIII, 22) in attributing great importance to this catastrophe as a destroyer of religious spirit and discipline. At all events, though the friars had lost some of their original fervor before the Black Death, it offers a convenient boundary line, so that the period chosen for treatment in this study is designed to give a view of the English Franciscan movement in its natural growth and decline, and to enable us, therefore, to understand better its true significance.

In the preparation of this essay I am especially indebted to Professor F. M. Powicke, my supervisor and patient guide at Oxford University; to Dr. A. G. Little for personal suggestions and for his scholarly researches on which I have heavily drawn; to Mr. W. Pantin, M. A., of Oriel College, Oxford, and other members of the faculty of the university; to my superiors who made possible my work abroad; to my confreres in Oxford and elsewhere for their kind hospitality and cooperation; and to several of my students of history for assistance in reading proofs and preparing the index.

VICTOR G. GREEN, O. M. CAP.

St. Fidelis Seminary
Herman, Pennsylvania

I

THE NATURE AND SPREAD OF THE FRANCISCAN MOVEMENT

The mendicant movement[1] which swept over Europe during the early thirteenth century was the Church's long-delayed answer to insistent cries for internal reform. The religious revival inaugurated by the Cluniac monks in the tenth century had largely spent its force. The successors of Gregory VII were not as strong as Gregory had been, and they had not come out so well in their conflicts with civil rulers. It was the great achievement of Innocent III to have made the papacy at last triumphant. The Church was never so free to effect the sadly-needed revival of her spiritual life. The urgency of such a revival was brought home by the rapid spread of tenacious heresies, which, identifying the Church with her ministers and despairing of her power to eradicate the deep-seated evils sapping her vitality, attacked the doctrine of the Church as well as the laxity of her representatives.

Whatever may be said of the Church's earlier attitude toward such groups as the Humiliati and Waldenses, Innocent III had no illusions about the real evils of the age and their remedy. That excommunications or the sword of a Simon de Montfort were not the answer to the Albigensians and kindred groups, he was well aware; hence he sought, especially after 1198, to direct the mendicant movement into orthodox channels.[2] Hence, too, efforts at reform were put forth by the Fourth Lateran Council

1. While this essay deals specifically with the Franciscans, much of what is said applies also to the Dominicans and other mendicants.

2. See Grundmann, *Religioese Bewegungen im Mittelalter* (Berlin, 1935), pp. 70 *et seq.*, 100, 156, etc.

which he summoned in 1215. It was this Council which approved the life and work of Sts. Francis and Dominic and their followers. And though Innocent died before his high courage and ability could bring to the reform movement the same success which attended his struggle for temporal power, he had set in motion the forces which would give a new and vigorous impetus to right living and help to postpone for several centuries the breaking up of Christian unity.[3]

By the simple austerity of their lives and the zeal of their preaching and ministrations, the friars were to steal the thunder of the heretics and give the lie to the theory that the Church was moribund and corrupt to the roots. The sincerity, piety and disinterested charity of the friars appealed to all classes and united all in a renewed loyalty to the Mother Church which could produce such Christlike men. By the time Innocent III's successor, Honorius III, formally approved the Franciscan rule in 1223, the sons of St. Francis had spread to practically all the countries of Europe. As early as 1219 some five thousand of them had gathered from various parts for the famous Chapter of Mats in Assisi; and Cardinal Ugolino, the future Pope Gregory IX, had presided at the chapter.[4]

At this time missions were sent into France, Spain, Germany, Hungary and other parts. Francis himself headed a mission into Egypt where he sought to convert the Sultan.[5] The missions to Germany and Hungary failed because the friars, ignorant of the

---

3. This view of Innocent's approval of the friars, especially as regards England, is not shared by Mr. Richard Howlett, who writes that "had it been possible for the great Pope to have seen in these Islands the main divisions of the Church discrediting each other in the face of the laity with yearly increasing indecency, he would have recognized the fact that the friar had destroyed the possibility of that natural balance which years would assuredly have brought about between seculars and regulars, and had thus, in the great result, lost to the papacy a kingdom destined to be of primary importance in Europe." *Monumenta Franciscana,* II (Rolls Series, London, 1882), p. ix. The reader of these pages must form his own judgment as to which is the correct view.

4. Eccleston, *De adventu Fratrum Minorum,* edited by Little (Paris, 1909), p. 40; Father Cuthbert, *Life of St. Francis of Assisi* (London, 1912), pp. 218-25.

5. H. Boehmer, ed., *Chronica Jordani* (Paris, 1908), nos. 3-6.

language of the people, were mistaken for heretics and driven from the land.[6] The friars who went to France were also mistaken for Albigensians, and the Holy See found it necessary to issue letters for their identification and protection.[7] The mission to Spain and thence to Morocco produced the first martyrs of the young fraternity, and inspired the other brethren with even greater zeal to preach in heathen lands.[8]

The German, Caesar of Speyer, was given charge of the second mission to Germany in 1221,[9] and this time the success of the friars was truly marvelous. Dividing into groups, they went about their work so thoroughly and systematically that by 1239 Germany possessed three distinct provinces of Franciscans; and German friars were being sent into Bohemia, Hungary, Poland, Norway, and Dacia.[10] By the end of the fourteenth century there were nearly two hundred Franciscan houses in Germany alone.[11] As elsewhere, the friars stemmed the tide of heresies, especially in the commercial centers along the Rhine, preached crusades, acted as papal nuncios and collectors, and stirred all classes to new spiritual fervor.[12]

If not every country has supplied us with chronicles like Friar Jordan's delightful account of the German mission and Friar Thomas Eccleston's candid story of the first friars in England, we know nevertheless that they were early at work in every Christian land, as well as among the Tatars, Mohammedans and other in-

---

6. *Ibid.*, 5, 6.

7. *Bullarium Franciscanum,* I, 2 and 5. The first bull, *Cum dilecti filii,* was issued to all Christian prelates June 11, 1219; the second, *Pro dilectis filiis,* issued May 29, 1220, was an answer to the "scruples" of the French clergy, and refers to a former letter on the friars.

8. *Chronica Jordani,* 7; and note p. 7; Father Cuthbert, *Life of St. Francis,* pp. 238-40 and references.

9. *Chronica Jordani,* 16 *et seq.*

10. *Ibid.*, 21, 23, 55, etc.; Adolf Koch, *Die fruehesten Niederlassungen der Minoriten im Rheingebiet* (Leipzig, 1881), p. 118 and *passim.*

11. Luke Wadding, *Annales Minorum* (Quaracchi, 1931-1934), IX, 222-27.

12. *Chronica Jordani,* p. 17 *et seq.;* Koch, *op. cit., passim;* Dr. Karl Mueller, *Die Anfaenge des Minoritenordens und der Bussbruderschaften* (Freiburg, 1885), chap. IV, etc.

fidels.[13] Matthew Paris did not exaggerate when he wrote in the year 1244 that the preaching of the Dominicans and the Franciscans had gone forth "to the ends of the earth."[14]

It was in the year 1224 that the first Franciscans came to England. They had learned a lesson from their first attempts in Germany and Hungary, for among the nine friars who landed at Dover, England, on May 3, 1224,[15] were three native English clerics. Besides, Agnellus of Pisa, head of the English mission, had been custos in Paris and probably knew some French, while the five lay brothers may also have learned some French during their sojourn in France.[16] At all events, we hear of no language difficulties such as were experienced by members of even the second mission to Germany.[17] But the English missionaries also had their troubles. The Lanercost chronicler writes of the first nine to land at Dover, that they were "simple and despicable, for at that time all born fools differed hardly at all from them in their manner of dress."[18] Then he goes on to give examples of how despised they really were. On their arrival they sought hospitality at the house of a nobleman near Dover. He gave them a room, but when they had retired he locked them in, and the next morning brought them up for trial as spies and robbers. On hearing the charge made against them, one of the friars smilingly took off the cord with which he was girded and handed it to his accuser with the remark, "If you take us for men of such a character, here is a halter with which to hang us." The judges were impressed by this gesture and decided that men who so freely offered themselves to death could not be evildoers; and the friars were released in the presence of a crowd of curious onlookers.

---

13. See, for example, the materials gathered in G. Golubovich, *Biblioteca bio-bibliografica della Terra Santa* (Quaracchi, 1906-1930). 6 vols.

14. *Chronica major,* Rolls Series, IV, 346.

15. Eccleston gives September 10, 1224, as the date of their arrival. The Dominicans came in 1222.

16. Eccleston, *De adventu,* pp. 4-7.

17. *Chronica Jordani,* p. 27.

18. Edited by Stevenson (Edinburgh, 1839), pp. 30, 31.

The second incident related by the chronicler took place near Oxford shortly after the friars' settlement there. A certain knight hated the very sight of them and abused their good name wherever he could. Christmas was approaching and the superior sent the friars out two by two "to sow the saving seed of the Lord." As two of them were making their way through a neighboring wood, their naked feet left stains of blood upon the frozen ground and snow; but all unconscious of this, the younger friar asked his senior if he might lighten the journey by singing. On obtaining the permission he broke forth into the *Salve Regina.* When he had finished he asked his companion: "Brother, was not that well sung?" "Yes, by the Lord, it was," a strange voice interrupted; "and may it ever go well with you who are so patient in necessities and joyful in adversities!" It was the knight who had so hated their manner of life. Noticing their blood-stained footprints in the snow, he had been following them unobserved. Now he dismounted from his horse and knelt to beg their forgiveness, after which he took them to his home for refreshment, and remained their loyal friend and benefactor ever after.[19]

Similar stories are narrated elsewhere, and almost invariably there is the happy ending. It was the heroic age of the fraternity, and virtue was always triumphant in the end.[20] Nevertheless, the hardships and the heroism of the first English Franciscans were very real indeed. Eccleston tells of their traveling barefoot in winter, their poor huts and their meager fare. At Canterbury for a time they remained shut up during the day in a little room behind the schoolhouse. After the scholars had gone home in the evening, they would make a fire in the school and gather about it. Sometimes they would heat the dregs of ale in a pot over the fire and dip out the unsavory drink with a cup which was

---

19. *Ibid.,* p. 31.

20. There is the story of Friar Robert of Ware whose father opposed his joining the friars. See article by G. R. Owst in *Dublin Review,* April, 1925, pp. 382-84; also the story of Richard Gobiun. Eccleston's *Chron.,* pp. 29, 30.

passed around to each in turn. If the ale became too thick, they added water; and they drank it with great joyfulness.[21] At Salisbury it was much the same, while in London the ale was frequently so sour that many of the brethren preferred to drink water. And they ate bread which was commonly called *torta,* a sort of rye bread, if they were so fortunate as to have even that.[22]

But whatever the hardships, there is always and everywhere the dominating note of Franciscan joyfulness, not only when the brethren drank their sour ale, but also in the refectory and choir when they should have been recollected. The young Oxford friars seem to have been particularly given to laughter, so much so that one of them, to cure himself, had to have recourse to taking the discipline every time he laughed in the choir or the refectory. He scourged himself eleven times in one day without results.[23] This joyfulness, for all its apparent excess in the case of the Oxford friar, was combined with a genuine religious spirit,[24] and the two undoubtedly did much to ingratiate the friars with the people. They made friends rapidly, and Eccleston expressly declares that "as the number of the brethren increased and their sanctity became known, the devotion of the people toward them increased likewise, so that they provided them eagerly with suitable dwellings."[25]

It was especially the townsmen who took the friars to their heart. The earliest sites and friaries were provided largely by the burgher class or by the lesser nobility; and the friars held the property, in keeping with their vow of poverty, at the will of the citizens who continued to own it. This was certainly the case with the properties at Canterbury, London and Oxford, the three first foundations,[26] and most probably remained the practice till some-

---

21. Eccleston, pp. 8, 9.
22. *Ibid.,* pp. 9-11. On *torta,* see *The Bread of Our Forefathers,* W. J. Ashley (Oxford, 1928), p. 152.
23. Eccleston, p. 32.
24. *Ibid.,* pp. 30-32 and *passim.*
25. *Ibid.,* p. 25.
26. *Ibid.,* pp. 25-81.

time during the fourteenth century.[27] William of Benington, subdean of Lincoln, granted land to the Franciscans in that town, but in 1231 the townsmen added to it and held it in their own name.[28] At Reading the friars held their property at the will of the monks,[29] at Northampton at the will of a particular benefactor, a knight.[30] The townsmen of Cambridge first received the friars there and assigned them temporarily an old synagogue near the prison.[31] Later the king provided a better place.[32] Townsmen were the principal benefactors of the convent at Beverley.[33] At Scarborough, the townsmen granted a spring to Robert the Dean so that he could provide the friars with water by means of a conduit.[34] Merchants of the steelyard were considered the founders of the Boston convent.[35] The bailiffs granted land to the friars at Bridgewater.[36] And so the evidence could be multiplied.[37]

The friars were anxious to have it understood that they did not own what was turned over to them. In 1280 King Edward licensed the Franciscans of Salisbury to receive gifts of land and houses from friends whose property adjoined the friars' site, "as the king understands that they have no property but only the use in donatives."[38] As it was a friar who insisted on the use of such language by the king,[39] one is inclined to think that the friars were by this time beginning to "protest too much." Still, the

---

27. The next paragraph tells how the friars insisted on it in 1280. In 1321 the king demanded that the deeds relating to Franciscan properties in London be turned over to the friars in order to avoid disorder and difficulties. *Cal. Close, 1318-1323,* p. 487 (Aug. 26, 1321). How general the practice became I do not know.

28. *Patent Rolls, Hen. III, 1225-1232,* pp. 422-3.

29. Eccleston, pp. 99, 100.

30. *Ibid.,* pp. 29, 30.

31, 32. *Ibid.,* p. 28.

33. *Victoria County Histories,* Yorks., III, 265.

34. *Ibid.,* II, 274.

35. *Ibid.,* Lincolnshire, II, 215.

36. *Cal. Patent Rolls, 1232-1247,* p. 470.

37. See, for example, A. G. Little, *Studies in English Franciscan History* (Manchester, 1917), pp. 6-8, 46 *et seq.*

38. *Cal. Pat., 1272-1281,* p. 392.

39. *English Historical Review,* 1934, pp. 673 *et seq.*

fact remains, as we shall see, that they clung remarkably close to their ideal of poverty until after the period here treated. As with their property, so with their daily sustenance, the friars depended on the charity of the people. Friar Martin de Barton, first custos of York, would permit none of the friaries in his custody to have more members than could be supported by alms alone.[40] Because he feared that it would burden his people if both Dominicans and Franciscans founded convents in Chester, Alexander, Bishop of Lichfield, at first opposed the settlement of the Franciscans in that town. Bishop Grosseteste, however, assured his brother bishop that Providence would never allow the necessary alms to fail, and that for the alms they gave the people would be amply recompensed by the spiritual ministrations of the friars.[41]

We are not immediately concerned here with the question whether this dependence upon alms was ultimately for good or evil. Dr. Little, who discusses the problem at length, arrives at the "general conclusion that the necessity of maintaining themselves on alms impaired the social usefulness of the friars, and their spiritual force. The pressure of material needs was too insistent. The cares of poverty proved as exacting and distracting as the cares of property."[42] But Dr. Little admits that "this dependence on alms certainly kept them poor; it kept them in touch with all classes in the country; it kept constantly alive the feeling of dependence on others; it promoted courtesy and humility."[43] And these things, we believe, were of the utmost importance both in the social usefulness and in the spiritual force of the Franciscans. The heroic lives and work of Franciscans all through history are somehow inseparable from St. Francis' peculiar devotion to Lady Poverty. Both Franciscan spirituality and Franciscan

---

40. Eccleston, p. 44.
41. *Roberti Grosseteste epistolae,* Rolls Series, pp. 120-22.
42. *Studies,* p. 91. See also discussion, *ibid.,* pp. 55-91.
43. *Ibid.,* p. 46.

charity depend upon it, and each new revival of the Franciscan spirit (the Observant and Capuchin reforms, for example) was a harking back to a more primitive Franciscan poverty. The Franciscan Rule insists on poverty rather than mendicancy, though St. Francis certainly thought mendicancy good for the soul. He wisely preferred to allow his friars to beg when the wages of their work were not given to them,[44] rather than have them exposed to the risk of attachment to any kind of property. Looking at it from a worldly-wise point of view, particularly if one places too much emphasis upon the evils associated with begging friars of the later and degenerate type, Dr. Little's verdict seems not unreasonable; but when one has seen the measurable good which the friars accomplished as long as they kept close to St. Francis' ideal, to say nothing of those spiritual or supernatural influences which elude human computation, it is difficult to believe that begging really "impaired the social usefulness of the friars, and their spiritual force." The harm came rather from the abuse of begging, as the ideal of poverty became more and more obscured.

Before attempting a brief survey of the Franciscan conquest of England, it is necessary to cast a glance at the conditions which prevailed at the time of their arrival. Unlike most of the continental countries, England of the thirteenth century had very few heretics. Her population of two or three millions was wholly Catholic.[45] However, as elsewhere, the clergy in England left much to be desired. Many were uneducated or morally unfit for the care of souls; and the system of farming and appropriating churches, with its consequent absentee rectors and poorly paid curates, was not designed to bring the best men to the fore. The control of so many parish churches by large monasteries, which

---

44. Testament of St. Francis. Cf. Paschal Robinson, *The Writings of St. Francis of Assisi* (Philadelphia: The Dolphin Press, 1906), p. 83.

45. See H. Grundmann, *Religioese Bewegungen,* p. 22, n. on suspected heretics who came from Flanders in 1160 and were tried at an Oxford synod; *ibid.,* p. 33, and Migne, *Patrologia Latina,* vol. 190, cols. 935-6, for letters of Gilbert Foliot, Bishop of London, to Roger, Bishop of Worcester (1164-1170), warning him against heretics among the weavers who were preaching their doctrines to the crowd.

hired the clerks or appointed the vicars who served them, while preferable to lay control, did not eliminate the evils of a bad system. Nor did it make for friendly relations between the monks and the reforming friars.[46] The monks themselves, despite their great missionary work of an earlier day, were not intended for the care of souls. This was not the purpose of their organization, and by the thirteenth century they had pretty generally withdrawn to the contemplative life, leaving the people in charge of curates who too often lacked both spirituality and practical efficiency. There was a crying need for men like the friars to fill up the gap between the contemplative monks and the too worldly clerics. Combining the contemplative with the active life in a truly evangelical manner, the friars set higher standards for the monks and clergy as well as for the people. They demonstrated how the contemplative and the active might be combined unto self-sanctification and the good of others. That is why the saintly Bishop Grosseteste took to them so kindly, and that is why they were everywhere so beloved of the people.[47]

Though perhaps the richest European country of the Middle Ages, and possessed of a feudal system not unlike that which existed on the greater part of the continent, England was not free from the problems of poverty and overcrowded and unsanitary towns. She did have an admirable system of hospitals and lazar-houses, founded and endowed by kings, princes and bishops;[48] and monasteries as well as episcopal and baronial households made regular provision for pilgrims and paupers. Flourishing guilds among the crafts and trades provided for their members and families in distress. But there must have been a large un-

---

46. On conditions in the English Church, see F. S. Stevenson, *Robert Grosseteste* (London, 1899), pp. 126-46, 151-53, *and passim;* also G. R. Owst, *Preaching in Medieval England* (Cambridge, 1926), pp. 10-55.

47. See this essay, chap. II *passim.*

48. See R. M. Clay, *The Medieval Hospitals of England* (London, 1909).

provided-for dependent class which eked out a miserable existence in the unhealthy slums.[49]

There was much work for the friars to do among these, for they were the type among whom heresies had spread so rapidly on the continent. And whether we accept Prof. Brewer's view[50] that the English Franciscans deliberately chose sites for their crude friaries in order to be among the wretched poor of the suburbs, or Dr. Little's[51] that the friars were guided by no general principle but accepted such sites as were given them, it still holds good that they settled among the people, mostly near the town walls and often in unhealthy places, where their services were most needed, and not in "splendid isolation" on some large estate.[52]

Finally, England on the arrival of the friars, though not torn as were Italy and Germany by wars between petty city states or by the conflict between Pope and Emperor, was experiencing a great deal of political unrest because of differences between the king and his barons. King John had issued the *Magna Carta* and made promises of freedom and justice to his people, but it was quite another matter for his successors to remain faithful to these promises. Troubles between the king and the barons were to come to a head again under the weak and arbitrary rule of Henry III, and in this struggle the Franciscans were to play an important rôle, just as they were to play an important part in almost every

---

49. *The Calendar of Liberate Rolls, 1240-1245,* pp. 124, 306, 324, etc., has such items as these: royal alms to feed 50,000 poor in Oxford and Ospring; 50,000 in London and elsewhere; 2,000 at Ankerwick an Bromhal; 15,000 in St. Paul's Churchyard, London; 10,000 others in London, etc.

50. *Monumenta Franciscana,* I, pp. xvii-xix.

51. *Studies,* pp. 10, 11.

52. *Ibid.,* pp. 10-13. St. Bonaventure, *Opera omnia,* VIII (Quaracchi, 1898), Opusculum XIII, Quaestio V, pp. 340-41, discusses the question of friaries and friary sites at length, and gives three principal reasons why the Franciscans settled in cities and towns: 1) edification — in order to be on hand when required by the people for confession, instructions, etc.; 2) the necessity of providing the food and other requirements of the friars, not so easily obtainable in the country; 3) protection — against those who might wish to steal the sacred vessels, etc., against people who might be offended by a sermon or because a member of their family came to the friars contrary to their will, etc.

other phase of medieval English life. Nor was this strange to the medieval mind which accepted "a hierarchy of values, embracing all human interests and activities in a system of which the apex is religion," contrasted with the modern view of society with its "conception of separate and parallel compartments, between which a due balance should be maintained, but which have no vital connection with each other."[53] As apostles of a revived and purified conception of Christian living, the Franciscans sought to leaven the whole mass of men. Impelled by a burning zeal and guided by a simple, direct vision, they let no class distinctions, forms or conventions stand in the path of their goal of bringing all men closer to Christ, Whom they sought to reproduce as far as might be in their own lives.

As long as they were fired by this consuming love of the Crucified and the souls redeemed by Him, neither the frosts and snows of England nor the the coldness of human indifference and opposition could stay their victorious march. When this internal flame began to burn low and men began to notice a discrepancy between the doctrine they preached and the lives they led, their charm and influence diminished too. By the time of Wyclif, Chaucer and Langland, the first heroic age had passed; the Reformation cut short the English Franciscan revival led by the Observants, though it was begun anew soon after with headquarters at Douai. But here we are dealing with the first age, and we return now to the story of how the first Franciscans took possession of England.

Though they landed at Dover, the Franciscans seem never to have established a house there. Whether the inhospitable treatment they received on landing had anything to do with this is a matter on which we can only speculate. Having crossed over from France at the expense of the monks of Fécamp, it is possible that they had a letter of introduction to the Prior of Christ Church,

53. R. H. Tawney, *Religion and the Rise of Capitalism* (London, 1926), p. 8.

Canterbury, who showed them hospitality for two days.[54] Then, while four of their number went on to London, the other five found refuge in a priests' hospital, whence they later moved to the little room behind the schoolhouse.[55] Before long they made many prominent friends in Canterbury, among them Archdeacon Simon Langton, brother of the famous archbishop, and a certain noble recluse, Loretta, Countess of Leicester, through whose influence they won the good-will of prelates and princes.[56]

The group which went on to London were kindly received by the Dominicans, with whom they stayed for fifteen days, until they were able to hire a house in Cornhill from a townsman by the name of John Travers. In this house they made themselves cells and stuffed the cracks with grass. A lay brother, Henry the Lombard, became the first guardian, while the two clerics who belonged to the mission, Richard of Ingeworth and Richard of Devon, remained only till the end of October and proceeded to Oxford. Here the Dominicans were again their hosts, putting them up for eight days until they were able to hire a house in the parish of St. Ebbe from Robert le Mercer. This house they later deserted for another which was given to the town for their use by Richard le Muliner.[57] At Oxford the friars "sowed the mustard seed of the sweet Jesus" and soon received reënforcements. Friars Richard of Ingeworth and Richard of Devon moved on to Northampton, leaving the novice, William of Esseby, as the first guardian of the Oxford house.[58] At Northampton the friars were first received into a hospital; then they hired a house in the parish of St. Giles. Peter the Spaniard became the first guardian

54. Eccleston, pp. 7, 8.

55. *Ibid.*, p. 8.

56. *Ibid.*, pp. 25-6. On Countess Loretta, the noble recluse of Hackington (a mile north of Canterbury), see F. M. Powicke's essay in *Historical Essays in Honour of James Tait* (Manchester, 1933), pp. 247-72. Loretta was related by marriage to the De Montfort family, whose relations with the Franciscans are discussed in chap. III of this essay.

57. Eccleston, pp. 11-13 and 27-8.

58. *Ibid.*, pp. 12, 13.

there, so that we are left to infer that the two Richards continued their work of founding friaries in other towns.[59] As Englishmen and clerics, they were probably best fitted for dealing with the townsmen and making the necessary friends among them.[60]

As the work progressed, recruits from across the sea evidently came to the aid of the first nine. Peter the Spaniard was one of these. Thomas of Spain and Henry Misericorde, first guardians of Cambridge and Lincoln respectively, were others.[61] But it was not long before native Englishmen began to join the order. The first novice to be received was the famous Friar Salomon, whose own sister turned her back on him when, as procurator of the brethren, he came to her home to beg. Salomon was a very strict observer of poverty. He used to collect only what was absolutely necessary for the sick brethren he served, carrying salt, figs, flour and the like in his caperone and firewood under his arm. On one occasion he himself suffered so much from cold that he thought he was dying. His brethren had nothing wherewith to warm him, but "holy charity suggested to them a remedy"; all of them, namely, huddled about Salomon "as is the custom of pigs" and thus kept him warm. Later Salomon suffered severe ailments contracted from going barefoot in the snow, but he nevertheless became guardian of the London friary and "general confessor of the whole city." On his deathbed he had scruples about his leniency with the rich who came to him as penitents.[62]

The second novice was William of London. He was of the household of Hubert de Burgh, the justiciar, and was renowned as a tailor. After him came Brother Joyce of Cornhill; then

---

59. *Ibid.*, p. 13. Richard of Ingeworth was later custodian of Cambridge and provincial minister of Ireland. He died as a missionary in Palestine. Eccleston, pp. 4, 5; A. G. Little, *The Grey Friars in Oxford* (Oxford, 1892), p. 178. Richard of Devon also traveled to other lands, and both were considered exemplars of virtue and zeal. Eccleston, p. 5.

60. The German, Caesar of Speyer, was selected for the German mission. *Chronica Jordani,* no. 19.

61. Eccleston, p. 13.

62. *Ibid.*, pp. 15-18.

Brother John, who died young; Brother Philip, a London priest, who became guardian at Bridgenorth and did great work as a preacher. These were followed by a number of university masters who increased the fame of the brethren. Best known among them is perhaps Adam Marsh, of whom we shall hear more later.[63] In 1235 John of Reading, Augustinian Abbot of Osney, joined the Franciscans,[64] and four years later Ralph of Maidstone, Bishop of Hereford, was also received into the order.[65] Knights, too, entered their ranks,[66] and the number of friars became so great that houses had to be enlarged and new ones built.[67]

By 1256, thirty-two years after the arrival of the first Franciscans in England, their number had grown to 1,242 friars, dwelling in forty-nine houses.[68] A comparison of a list of these foundations with a map of England shows that they were situated in virtually every section of the country, especially in the more important centers. In the southeast there were such places as London, Salisbury, Canterbury, Southampton, Lewes, Winchester and Chichester. In the southwest were Bristol, Exeter, Gloucester, Hereford and Bridgewater. More centrally located were the places attached to the Oxford custody, namely: Oxford, Reading, Bedford, Stamford, Nottingham, Northampton and Leicester. To the east were Cambridge, Norwich, Colchester, Ipswich and King's Lynn. To the northwest were Worcester, Coventry, Lichfield, Shrewsbury, Chester, Llanfaes in Wales and Bridgenorth. To the northeast were York, Lincoln, Grimsby and Scarborough. In the custody of Newcastle to the extreme north were Newcastle, Har-

---

63. *Ibid.*, pp. 20-24. For brief biographies of Adam Marsh, Adam of Oxford, Richard Rufus and other famous Franciscan scholars, see *Grey Friars in Oxford*, pp. 125-294. On Adam Marsh, see also chap. III of this essay.

64. Eccleston, p. 24 and note: *Annales monastici*, R. S., IV, 82; *Grey Friars in Oxford*, pp. 180-81.

65. Eccleston, p. 107 and references; *Monumenta Franciscana*, R. S., I, 542; *Grey Friars in Oxford*, p. 182.

66. Eccleston, p. 24.

67. *Ibid.*, pp. 25-30, 54-59.

68. *Ibid.*, p. 14.

tlepool, Carlisle; and in Scotland, Berwick, Roxburgh and Haddington.[69]

This list comprises most of the centers established before 1256. There were others, and more were to follow. But by this time the first great burst of enthusiasm was on the wane, and opposition on the part of the monks and others was gathering force. There was increasing need, too, of bringing this free-lance invasion more within the ordinary parochial organization of the country, and of imposing upon the greatly increased number of friars a greater rigidity of internal discipline. While larger houses and communities of friars would probably make for more regular monastic observance, it naturally lessened the mobility of the Franciscan forces. Shall we call this something of a necessary evil?[70] In spite of the year's novitiate required before a candidate could become a full-fledged Franciscan,[71] such a rapid increase of members as took place in England would in the very nature of things lead to the admission of some untried and unworthy members. And the work which the friars were called upon to do, together with the remarkable freedom of their movement about the country in the early days, was full of temptation.[72] It is therefore not surprising that some of the weaker brethren succumbed, to the scandal of the faithful and the injury of the young fraternity's reputation. Eccleston tells us that even one of the pioneers, Henry the Lombard, who began to learn letters by studying at night after he had been made guardian of the London friary, was

---

69. See Appendix I for list of Franciscan houses. It was only from 1331 to 1359 that the Scottish Franciscans formed a separate province. Moir Bryce, *The Scottish Grey Friars* (Edinburgh, 1909), pp. 9-13.

70. St. Bonaventure (*Opera omnia,* VIII, pp. 367-8) gives religious discipline as his first reason in justification of larger houses. Others are study, devotion, service of the people, training of novices, etc.

71. *Bullarium Franciscanum,* I, 6, bull *Cum secundum,* Sept. 22, 1220.

72. See, for example, Friar Salimbene's gossipy account of his travels and those of his confrères. *Cronica Fratris Salimbene de Adam,* in *Monumenta Germaniae Historica,* XXXII (Hannover, 1905). Jacques de Vitry, writing as a friendly outsider, speaks of the dangers in a mode of life in which untried youths were sent out two and two "through the whole world." Cf. letter quoted by Father Cuthbert in his *Life of St. Francis,* p. 245.

unable to bear his honors and miserably apostatized from the order.[73] There were other similar cases, which certainly did the friars no good.[74] As early as 1249, the king gave orders to "all bailiffs and others to take when called upon by the Friars Minor all persons clerical or lay whom the Friars Minor shall testify to be apostates of their order, and to commit them to the king's prison, or if the said friars prefer, deliver them to the friars."[75] Henry III probably had these difficulties in mind when on one occasion he cautioned the friars about the kind of candidates they should receive. Hearing that certain knights had entered the order, the king remarked to the brethren: "If you will be discreet in the reception of friars, will not procure privileges to the injury of others, and especially if you will not be importunate in begging, you will be able to rule over princes."[76]

To a degree it might be said that the Franciscan ideal was obscured by its very popularity. I do not mean in the sense that every ideal translated into practice loses the character of an ideal, but in the sense that the weight of untried numbers in pursuit of it dragged it down. St. Francis himself had realized the moral impossibility of maintaining the high standards he had set for his followers, once their numbers became great, and concessions and allowances had to be made for weaker brethren. Therefore on one occasion he had exclaimed in bitterness of soul: "Oh that it might be that the world, seeing Friars Minor but rarely, would wonder at their fewness!"[77] The marvel is that Francis' ideal could have been preserved so well and so long in spite of the number of its would-be adherents. It is, therefore, not surprising that the tempo of the English apostolate slowed down consider-

73. Eccleston, pp. 13, 14: compare *ibid.,* p. 7. See also *ibid.,* p. 38 and note, and this essay, chap. IV, on the friars who lived in courts, etc.

74. This essay, chaps. IV and V.

75. *Cal. Pat., 1247-1258,* p. 48. The early German friars also had trouble with apostates. *Chronica Jordani,* 35.

76. Eccleston, p. 24.

77. Celano, *S. Francisci Assisiensis vita et miracula,* II, 70, edition of Edouard d'Alencon (Rome, 1906), pp. 224-5.

ably after 1256, when the houses numbered forty-nine and the friars 1,242.

The peak of membership, however, was not reached till the close of the period with which we are dealing, that is, about 1348, when the Black Death began its terrible assault upon all classes of the population.[78] At this time the English Franciscan friaries numbered fifty-eight and the friars approximately 2,000.[79] The largest house, London, had ninety friars in 1336. Oxford was next in size, with eighty-four friars in 1317. At Cambridge the number varied between fifty-five in 1289 and seventy in 1338. At York there were from thirty-six to fifty-two; at Winchester, from twenty-eight to forty-three; and so on down to the small Scottish friaries of four or five members. The numbers often varied in the same house during the course of a particular year, one friary gaining what another lost.[80]

The distribution of friaries was much the same as in 1256. Apart from the extension of the provincial limits northward and westward farther into Scotland and Wales, it was largely a matter of filling up the gaps between houses by foundations at such places as Stafford, Preston, Beverley, Doncaster, Boston, Richmond, Grantham, Dorchester, Yarmouth, Dunwich, etc.[81] In 1385 the number of friaries was given as sixty,[82] but it is unlikely that the number of friars ever again attained the 2,000 mark, even though the latter part of the fourteenth century was a period of great popularity for the Franciscans. Many notables came to them and

---

78. See Gasquet's *The Black Death.* For estimates of the damage to the Franciscans, see E. Hutton, *The Franciscans in England, 1224-1538* (London, 1926), pp. 172-80; the Bodmin Franciscan chronicle quoted in Sir John Maclean, *The Parochial and Family History of the Deanery of Trigg Minor* (London, 1873), I, 190; Wadding, *Annales Minorum,* VIII, 22.

79. Dr. Little's painstaking calculation, *Studies,* pp. 68-70.

80. *Ibid., loc. cit.* London had eighty friars as early as 1242, judging from the king's gift to them of eighty tunics on December 9 of that year. *Cal. Liberate Rolls, 1240-1245,* p. 204. A year earlier Winchester had twenty-three friars. *Ibid.,* p. 144.

81. See list, Appendix I.

82. Bartholomew of Pisa's list, *Analecta Franciscana,* IV, 545-47.

they figured very strongly in wills and bequests from all classes.[83] Despite the denunciations of Wyclif and his followers, it must be remembered that the leaders of the Peasants' Revolt of 1381 had planned to spare only the mendicants in their attack upon civil and ecclesiastical overlords.[84] But too great popularity had much to do with injuring the religious spirit of the friars and weakening their love of poverty, the backbone of the Franciscan rule. Add to this the inferior character of the candidates who came to fill up the vacancies caused by the Black Death,[85] and we have perhaps the chief external causes of the Franciscan decline.[86]

It must not be thought, however, that the English Franciscans ever became great property-holders. The reports of Henry VIII's investigators at the Dissolution are evidence of the universal poverty of the Franciscan houses compared with many of the large monasteries of the monks.[87] Still, the Patent Rolls after 1300 show an increasing tendency among the Franciscans and other mendicants to add to their properties. The Black Death increased the ease with which property could be acquired and accelerated the tendency; although, as Miss K. L. Wood-Legh points out, the holdings of the mendicants were never large. And the Franciscans, despite the fact that they were undoubtedly the most popular of the mendicants and also the most numerous, seem to have taken least advantage of the opportunity to enrich themselves.[88] In 1349 the king ordered an investigation of an alleged practice which had grown up among the mendicants of acquiring

---

83. C. L. Kingsford, *The Grey Friars of London* (British Society of Franciscan Studies — B. S. F. S. — Aberdeen, 1915), p. 18: Little, *Grey Friars in Oxford,* pp. 100 *et seq.,* 239; *Wills and Inventories* (London: Surtees Society, 1835), II, pp. 6 *et seq.,* 32, etc.

84. Jack Straw's confessions, Walsingham, *Historia Anglicana,* II, 10 (Rolls Series).

85. Wadding's explanation, *Annales,* VIII, 22.

86. E. Hutton, *The Franciscans in England, 1224-1538,* pp. 236 *et seq.*

87. Dugdale, *Monasticon Anglicanum* (London, 1825), vol. VI, part III, pp. 1509-1545; *Grey Friars in Oxford,* pp. 112-24.

88. *Church Life in England under Edward III* (Cambridge, 1934), pp. 78-83.

properties and houses and renting them to laymen, "whereas they ought to live by begging according to their rule."[89] This investigation, Dr. Little thinks, was probably part of Richard Fitzralph's movement against the friars; and, after studying the available reports of the royal investigators, he decides that "the conclusion to be drawn from them is that all four orders in England down to 1350 lived on alms and not on rents. The exceptions are so insignificant that they may be disregarded."[90]

Miss Wood-Legh summarizes her findings regarding the four orders of mendicants for the reign of Edward III in these words: "On the whole, the impression left, after one has examined all the licenses and pardons that concern the friars, is that their possessions in land were extremely modest compared with those of even the most poorly endowed houses of the possessionist orders. If the friars were rich, they must have become so through direct gifts in money or in kind; yet even in their acquisitions of land, we see that the friars had considerably relaxed the rule of poverty under which their predecessors of the early thirteenth century had lived."[91] This is in agreement with Mr. Kingsford's judgment on the same period that "we are justified in believing that the good repute of the friars had up to this time little diminished, even though there had been some falling off from the zeal and strict observance of earlier times."[92]

As far as the Franciscans were concerned, Archbishop Pecham as well as St. Bonaventure saw the necessity of larger and more substantial houses, though both were strict devotees of poverty and certainly did not favor luxuries and superfluities.[93] As more and more restrictions came to be placed upon the friars in the use of parish churches for preaching, it was but natural that their own churches were built larger to accommodate the crowds who

89. *Cal. Fine Rolls,* VI, 181 and 226.
90. *Historical Essays in Honour of James Tait,* pp. 179-88.
91. *Church Life in England under Edward III,* p. 83.
92. *The Grey Friars of London,* p. 19.
93. This essay, chap. v.

flocked to hear them.[94] Writing about the middle of the fifteenth century, Bishop Reginald Pecock justified the ample churches of English mendicants, as long as they were not too ornate and costly, on the grounds "that ther bi the more multitude of persoones mowe be receyued togidere for to here theryn prechingis to be mad in reyne daies"; the crowds could also be "more eesid in her deuociouns," and might come to church on rainy days after midday to talk with friends and wise counsellors "aboute making of accordis and about redressing of wrongis and aboute othere vertuose deedis."[95]

More spacious friaries and churches, while perhaps necessary adaptations to time and circumstance, seemed to symbolize somewhat the decline in things of the spirit. As already indicated, the secret of the Franciscan success was mainly personal sanctity and devotion to an ideal. As examples of Christian living, the friars were a challenge to the laxity of their day and won the admiration and respect of men of good-will. As able exponents of the sweet charity of the Gospel, they in turn became the recipients of much well-meant charity and hero worship. And the more they succumbed to this and ceased to be so greatly different from the world in which they moved, the more their efficacy diminished. They might still go on doing excellent work, still preach "to make us for our olde synnes wepe";[96] but by the end of our period a more or less routine life and work had replaced the heroism and daring which filled the pages of earlier Franciscan annals. It is to these earlier records that we now return.

---

94. See H. E. Goad's account of the growth of larger Franciscan churches in Italy, *Franciscan Italy* (London, 1926), pp. 194-5.

95. *The Repressor of Over-Much Blaming of the Clergy,* Rolls Series (R. S.), pp. 553-4. The bishop also justifies mansionlike monastic buildings, especially those of the monks; *ibid.,* pp. 548-53.

96. *Canterbury Tales,* "Clerkes Tale," pp. 11-13.

II

THE FRIARS AND THE CROWD

Practically every phase of medieval Franciscan activity had some ultimate relation to the masses. Whether the friar used his good offices to promote peace between warring rulers, raised by his example and devotion to education the standard of clerical living and efficiency, helped to make articulate the growing popular demand for constitutional liberty, or personally preached to the people and ministered to their spiritual and material needs, there was always the practical goal of re-leavening society with the Gospel principles. And in such a revived Christian society the common man, the oppressed, the "little ones," had certainly most to gain. In the present chapter, however, we shall confine our attention to those more direct relations between the English Franciscans and the medieval "man in the street" — the townsmen, craftsmen and tradesmen, villeins and serfs, criminals and "floaters," and their wives and children. What did the friar do to deserve the love and devotion of these? Why did they welcome him and maintain him in preference to all other clergy and religious?[1]

First of all and basically, let us repeat, it was the sincerity and heroic life of the first Franciscans which called forth the admiration of men, their preaching by example as St. Francis had commanded them to do. People will soon perceive and fall in love with the genuine, the selfless, the daring. That is why Eccleston says that as "their sanctity became known, the devotion of the people toward them increased."[2] We have already told

1. See, for example, Jack Straw's confessions in Walsingham, *Historia Anglicana,* R. S., II, 10.
2. *Op. cit.,* p. 25.

how these ascetic sons of the Poverello went barefoot even in winter, drank sour ale and ate such simple fare as they could beg. Eccleston further assures us of the devotion with which they recited the Divine Office and practised meditation, sometimes spending the whole night in prayer.[3] Such was their love for Franciscan poverty and religious observance that the Minister General, John of Parma, wished to place the English Province "in the center of the world" as an example to all.[4] The missionary zeal of the friars was but the flowering of their own spirituality, the overflow of their own love for the Word Made Flesh. Hence in the early days, "friars who were of noble birth or for other reasons notable before the world and respected in the order allowed themselves to be sent to places which nowadays are called desolate."[5]

"They illuminate our whole country with the bright light of their preaching and teaching," wrote Bishop Grosseteste to Pope Gregory IX in 1238. "Their most holy conversation gives a powerful impetus to contempt of the world and to voluntary poverty, to humility even among those in high places, to entire obedience to prelates and the head of the Church, to patience in tribulation, to abstinence in the midst of plenty, in short, to every virtue. Oh that Your Holiness could see how devoutly and humbly the people run to hear from them the word of life, to confess their sins, to be instructed in the rules of living, and what advance the clergy and religious have made by imitating them; you would indeed say that 'to those that sit in the valley of the shadow of death the light hath shined.' "[6] "For the salvation of souls," according to the *Lanercost Chronicle*,[7] Grosseteste had the friars with him

---

3. *Ibid.,* p. 31.

4. *Ibid.,* p. 123, also pp. 86, 89, 91-2, 99.

5. *Ibid.,* pp. 32-3. See *Lanercost Chronicle,* pp. 68, 70, 71, 136, 186, etc., on the friars' reputation for holiness. While not excusing the friars of his day who from improper motives wished to neglect outlying places, St. Bonaventure gives a number of good reasons why they preferred ministering in the towns; *Opera omnia,* VIII, pp. 370-71.

6. *Epistolae,* p. 180.

7. P. 43.

constantly on his visitations of the diocese. They preached to the people and heard confessions while the bishop preached to the clergy, made investigations, effected reforms and confirmed the children.[8]

Similar praise and approval of the friars came from other dioceses. In 1266 Peter Quivil, Bishop of Exeter, spoke of the "inestimable fruit" accruing to souls from the work of the Franciscans and Dominicans in his diocese,[9] and in 1287 the Diocesan Statutes of Exeter decreed that the friars who passed through the diocese be well received and allowed to preach and hear confessions because of the good that they did.[10] In the same year like praise was bestowed and like orders were given by John le Romeyn, Archbishop of York.[11] In 1295 the synodal statutes of John de Pontissara, Bishop of Winchester, insisted that "no one subject to us shall prevent the Dominicans and Franciscans as they pass through the parishes, whether in Lent or at other times, from hearing the confessions of the faithful. . . . And since the preaching and holy conversation of the friars are known to bear no little fruit, we direct that when they pass through our diocese they shall be received everywhere with hospitality and respect."[12] Archbishop Wickwane reproached the Cistercians of Scarborough for refusing to allow these "most religious" Franciscans to preach in their parish, and empowered the friars in his diocese to absolve even certain reserved sins.[13]

The reason why the friars were so much in demand was not only that "there was no regular preaching," it being "left to the

---

8. *Lanercost Chronicle, loc. cit.;* Wharton, *Anglia Sacra* (London, 1691), p. 347 (Grosseteste's plan of diocesan visitation given before the Pope and the cardinals in 1250); see also Stevenson, *Robert Grosseteste,* pp. 130-31.

9. *Register,* edited by Hingeston-Randolf, p. 79.

10. Wilkins, *Concilia* (London, 1737), p. 134.

11. *Register,* Surtees Soc., vol. 123, pp. 67-8.

12. *Register,* Cant. and York Soc., vol. 19, pp. 209, 222. The wording is practically a repetition of the Exeter Statutes, above.

13. *Historical Papers and Letters from the Northern Registers,* R. S., p. 79; *Register* of Archbishop Wickwane, Surtees Soc., vol. 114, p. 317; for similar licenses see *Registers* of John de Pontissara (pp. 245-6), Peter Quivil, Walter de Stapelton, John de Grandisson, edited by Hingeston-Randolf.

friars on their rounds."[14] But even after the efforts of Bishop Grosseteste, Archbishop Pecham and others to correct the evil of little or no preaching among the seculars, the latter were often but poorly equipped for the task, whatever their good-will.[15] Visitors of the diocese of Exeter in 1301, for example, were informed by the parishioners of Colyton "that their vicar is an upright man and preaches to them as well as he knows how, but not sufficiently, they think. They also say that his predecessors used to call in the friars to instruct them in the salvation of their souls; but the present vicar does not care for the friars, and if they happen to come he will not receive them or show them hospitality. For which reason they petition that he be corrected."[16] On the other hand, though the visitor found other evils to be corrected, it was to the credit of the officials of Snaith, appropriated to Selby Abbey, "that the Friars Minor and Preachers often come and preach and are honorably received by the monks."[17]

The picture which the Episcopal Registers present rather vaguely of the friars on their rounds "passing through" the parishes, preaching and hearing confessions, is clarified somewhat by passages in Eccleston's chronicle, the *Lanercost Chronicle,* and other contemporary accounts, both friendly and hostile. The wandering life of the friars, their preaching and hearing of confessions everywhere in disregard of ancient convention and privilege, is a favorite theme of Matthew Paris and other hostile monastic chroniclers.[18] We have already referred to Eccleston's story of the Oxford friars sent out about Christmas "to sow the saving seed of the Lord in the land."[19] Similarly, the *Lanercost Chron-*

---

14. Bishop Hobhouse in Preface to *Register* of John de Drokensford (Somerset Rec. Soc., 1887), p. xxviii.

15. See A. G. Little, *Studies,* pp. 158 *et seq.*

16. From the archives of the dean and chapter of Exeter, printed in *Register* of Walter de Stapelton, p. 111.

17. *Register,* Arch. Giffard, Surtees Soc., Vol. 109, pp. 322-4.

18. See, e. g., Paris, *Chronica majora,* R. S., III, 332-4; IV, 279, 346; V, 529; *Historia Anglorum,* R. S., II, 110, 298-9; Roger Wendover, *Flores historiarum,* R. S., II, 35-6; *Memorials of St. Edmund's Abbey,* R. S., II, 264 *et seq.*

19. Eccleston, p. 31.

icle[20] tells of a preaching tour undertaken by the Dumfries Franciscans in Annandale. At other times we get glimpses of friars hurrying two and two, now practically unobserved, through a rural village to the north of London when a dying youth calls them to his bedside,[21] now arriving just in time to bring medicine and spiritual help to a dying miser (who, however, will have none of their ministrations and dies a terrible death),[22] or again seeming to be providentially guided to the deathbed of a heretic whom they insistently call upon to make his peace with God.[23]

Whatever the historical value of the details of some of these incidents, they help us to visualize the ubiquity of the medieval Franciscan and his intimate contact with his fellow-men. It is, of course, impossible to determine the number of these transient preachers and confessors engaged in the apostolate at any one time. But let us suppose that no more than half of the friars were so occupied during the chief preaching seasons of Lent and Advent. This would still give us from 500 to 1,000 friars operating from some forty to sixty centers all over the country. Suppose they went forth from these centers, preaching and instructing as they went, living on the alms of the people to whom they ministered — the territory they would cover in the course of a year would be extensive. And there would be comparatively few people in a population of two to three millions who would not at one time or other come under their influence.[24]

This influence would be wielded not only by good example and sermons, but in a more fruitful way by the confessional. Sermons and example might plant the seed of conversion and water it, but the fruit would be garnered in the closer intimacy of the tribunal of penance. It was here that the medicine of spiritual

---

20. Pp. 107-8.
21. *Ibid.,* pp. 70-1.
22. *Ibid.,* pp. 153-4.
23. *Ibid.,* pp. 188-9.
24. This does not include the work of the Dominicans and other friars engaged in the same field.

counsel and divine grace was applied to sick souls, virtue was encouraged and vice uprooted, and victories won over sin which are recorded only in the Book of Life. For it was precisely by her authority to bind the consciences of individuals that the medieval Church was able to effect some measure of justice and morality, some adherence to the principles of right living set forth in her teaching. Even if it happened that a bishop restricted the number of friar confessors in his diocese,[25] and none of them seems to have done so before 1300,[26] they would have been able to serve a considerable number of penitents at a time when frequent confession was unknown. In 1300 Bishop Dalderby licensed only about one-third of the Franciscans presented to him as confessors, and ultimately accepted fifty Franciscans and fifty Dominicans for the whole diocese of Lincoln. As there were nine Franciscan houses in the Lincoln diocese, out of a total of fifty-four in England and Wales, Dr. Little computes that, assuming similar action to have been taken by other bishops (for which we have no evidence), the number of Franciscan confessors would have been about 300.[27] Since the friar confessors were very popular, and many people who refused to go to their own priests went to the mendicants,[28] Franciscan influence through this means must have been considerable.

Even before priests became so predominant among the Franciscans, Eccleston speaks of "very many" confessors both to the religious and the laity, some of whom were famous.[29] Brother Salomon was confessor to the whole town of London, both to the courtiers and the ordinary citizen.[30] Other confessors of repute were Friar Maurice of Dereham; Friar Vincent of Worcester, who

---

25. See A. G. Little, *Studies,* pp. 115, 116.

26. *Ibid.,* p. 108, where Dr. Little gives what was perhaps the only instance of episcopal opposition to the Franciscans before 1300. And this opposition was only temporary.

27. *Ibid.,* pp. 115, 116 and note.

28. Matthew Paris, *Historia Anglorum,* R. S., II, 110.

29. Pp. 75-8.

30. *Ibid.,* 17 and 75.

became confessor to Roger de Wesham, Bishop of Lichfield and Coventry (1245-1256); Friar Godfrey of Salisbury; and Friar Eustace de Merc. All these were men of great sanctity and spiritual insight.[31] Matthew Paris, almost in the same breath in which he charges the friars with abusing their position by extorting wills and lying in wait at the deathbeds of the rich, admits that "none of the faithful any longer believe themselves to be saved unless they are guided by the counsels of the Preachers and the Minorites."[32] Archbishop Giffard insisted that the Carmelite nunneries in his jurisdiction should accept as their confessors the Franciscans "who shine in the Church of God as the brightness of the firmament."[33] There are many other instances of bishops of the thirteenth and fourteenth centuries demanding Franciscan confessors for the nuns in their dioceses.[34]

Naturally, it is not to be expected that any definite knowledge is available as to how the friars used the confessional, when so little remains by which to judge even the content of their sermons. They preached in the vernacular and probably, for the most part, never wrote the sermons.[35] Aside from so-called *Exempla,* or collections of illustrations and like materials for sermons, mostly written in Latin, we have little first-hand evidence of what the medieval English Franciscan told his interested audiences. The *Exempla,* however, and other works written by English Fran-

---

31. *Ibid.,* pp. 75-8.

32. *Chronica majora,* R. S., IV, 279. Paris' opinion of the mendicants seems to have mellowed considerably by the time he wrote his *Historia Anglorum,* of which work see R. S., II, 110, 298-9, 388; III, 94, 384, etc. On the unsubstantiated charges of Matthew Paris (*Chron. maj.,* IV, 279), Walsingham (*Hist. Angli.,* II, 13; *Chron. Angliae,* 1328-1388, p. 312), and others (*Fasciculus zizaniorum,* R. S., p. 294), that the friars abused the confessional, see Dr. Little, *Studies,* pp. 48, 114-22, etc.

33. *Register,* Surtees Soc., vol. 109, p. 295.

34. See A. G. Little, *Studies,* p. 119, note.

35. See Stevenson, *Robert Grosseteste,* p. 32; and Owst, *Preaching in Medieval England,* pp. 223-227, for explanation of why more sermons have not been preserved. It seems to have been the custom to write only the Latin sermons. The shortage of writing materials among the poor Franciscans would also help to explain the lack of sermon manuscripts from this source. See Little, *Grey Friars in Oxford,* pp. 91-2; *Monumenta Franciscana,* R. S., I, pp. lxi-ii, lxvii.

ciscans of the thirteenth and early fourteenth centuries for the guidance of clergy and laity,[36] especially the *Metaphors* or miniature sermons of Friar Bozon,[37] do give us a fairly good idea of the general trend of Franciscan preaching. From these evidences we are forced to the conclusion that the friars adhered pretty closely to St. Francis' admonition to preach "of vices and virtues, punishment and glory."[38] It is clear from them that the friars possessed a deep knowledge of human nature and were thoroughly acquainted with contemporary conditions. They were learned men, and possessed the art of making their learning popular, rousing their hearers' attention and driving home a point by apt illustrations and stories from Scripture, the Church Fathers, sacred and profane history, the ancient classics, the world of natural science, and the daily life and work of men. Friar Bozon's metaphors or parables are nearly all drawn from the animal world and applied with great ingenuity to all classes of men and all phases of Christian life. Oppressive lords, prelates and lawyers come in for a large share of reproach and admonition,[39] but the sins of the humbler classes are condemned with no less zeal. If the rich are flayed for greed, covetousness and oppression of the poor, the poor are warned to beware of ambition and other worldly allurements. Mutual charity, patience in adversity, justice, humility,

---

36. A. G. Little, ed., *Liber exemplorum,* British Society of Franciscan Studies, vol. I (Aberdeen, 1908), written for the use of preachers by an English Franciscan living in Ireland. See also Father J. Th. Welter, ed., *Speculum laicorum* (Paris, 1914); and *Fasciculus morum,* the proposed edition of which has not yet appeared. All of these, together with Friar Bozon, *Metaphors,* are discussed by Dr. Little, *Studies,* pp. 136 *et seq.*

Other works helpful in forming a judgment on medieval Franciscan preaching are *De proprietatibus rerum* by Friar Bartholomew the Englishman; and the *Summa collationum* of Friar John of Wales.

37. *Les contes moralises de Nicole Bozon Frère Mineur,* edited by Miss Lucy Toulmin Smith and M. Paul Meyer for the Société des Anciens Textes Francais (Paris, 1889). See Introduction on the authorship and the evidences showing that the sermons were used in England by a Franciscan of the early fourteenth century, though the language in which they were written is Norman-French. There is a less critical English translation by "J. R." entitled *The Metaphors of Brother Bozon* (London, 1913).

38. Franciscan Rule, chap. IX. Cf. Robinson, *Writings of St. Francis,* p. 71.

39. See Appendix III.

chastity, the meaning of the Incarnation and Passion of Christ, devotion to Mary, the value and need of confession and penance — these are the burden of Friar Bozon's interesting and forceful parables.[40]

Nowhere in the available Franciscan writings has the writer found an appeal to class hatred. Sin is everywhere condemned, virtue praised, and there is no respect of persons. Well might guilty lords and prelates wince under the fearless denunciation of their greed and injustice; but they were not condemned as a class, and their escape was to mend their ways. Nor is there any evidence in the writings that the friars sought to discredit the secular clergy or monks. In the *Liber exemplorum,* on the contrary, the author on a number of occasions gives explicit instructions to preachers that they should change a story which might scandalize the faithful by exposing the vices of religious persons. To illustrate the evil effects of gluttony, for instance, he gives the example of a monk who drank too much and eventually died in sin. At the end of the story he remarks that "it is not good to tell such things about religious persons to the people. But since he was indeed a man, the whole can be truthfully told about a certain man.... However, if you are preaching to religious, the whole story in its proper sequence will be useful."[41]

Some of the stories and illustrations may have been old or far-fetched, but they were nonetheless striking and captivating, well suited to relieve the monotony and boredom of religious instruction in an age when audiences were less sedate and less sophisticated than they are today. The medieval mind was not so skeptical about miracles and the nearness of the supernatural. Besides, the Crusades had whetted men's appetite for accounts of strange lands and happenings abroad. The popularity soon to be

40. See text, *passim;* also *English Popular Preaching in the Fourteenth Century,* by Lucy Toulmin Smith in *English Historical Review,* VII, 25-36.

41. A. G. Little, ed., *Liber exemplorum,* pp. 94-5. See also pp. xiii-xiv, 11, 56, 93-4, 98, 115-6, etc.

attained by such outlandish stories as those contained in Mandeville's *Travels* suggests the curiosity and gullibility of the age. The friar had, furthermore, to compete with the questionable entertainment and vulgar stories of wandering jesters and peddlers. Because he knew the temper of his listeners and was equipped to command their attention, he was successful in delivering his message. "Traveler, friend of the outcast, master alike of the ecclesiastical and the popular tongue, with an intimate knowledge of the world as well as of books, he could mingle in his discourse the latest 'narration' with the mysteries of nature, 'to please in method and invent by rule' — *joculator Dei* of St. Francis and sacred peddler rolled into one — forever bringing forth out of his treasure things old and new."[42]

To understand the distractions with which the medieval preacher had to contend, we must put aside our conception of a sedate and silent audience seated in comfortable pews. Remember that the friars often preached in the open air and to audiences composed largely of people who came and went at will, depending on whether they were entertained or bored. Or, if in church, the supposed listeners might sleep, quarrel, discuss business, interrupt the preacher with opinions of their own, or ask him questions, according to mood.[43]

It is not surprising, then, that friars resorted to "tricks of the trade" in order to command a hearing. Though pilloried in later times for appealing to the gallery, even the friar that Chaucer knew was not ineffective as a preacher.[44] One can see

---

42. G. R. Owst, *Preaching in Medieval England,* pp. 81-2.

43. Owst, *op. cit.,* pp. 157-184. In 1268 the king granted the Franciscans the use of a fosse belonging to the fortifications of York "in order to hold their preachings," on condition that they enclose it with a wall of earth and abandon it for defense in time of war. *Cal. Pat., 1266-1272,* pp. 260-261.

The *Lanercost Chronicle* gives the story of a loiterer at one of the Franciscan sermons who had come "more out of curiosity than for edification of soul" and stood "leaning against the wall." For objecting to the preacher's statements, he was cursed and suffered a violent death the same evening (p. 68).

44. See this essay, chap. I, p. 24 and reference.

in the *Exempla* and *Metaphors* the germ of possible abuse, but Wyclif's charge that the friars had recourse to novelties and rhymes[45] might really be a compliment as well as a reproach. What better to help the memory of an illiterate audience, for example, than a rhymed version of the Ten Commandments?[46] What better to rouse a sleepy audience or stop the hum of conversation among casual listeners than a good story? "Now and then the reader pictures the awakened congregation, eagerly leaning forward to catch some fragment of a traveler's reminiscence, as he describes the perils of the Italian roads, a vineyard custom in France he has observed, or some game which is 'commoner in parts beyond the sea.' "[47] If a decline in apostolic spirit later tended to convert a means to an end into an end in itself or into an instrument of cheap publicity and popularity, its invention and use by friars of a more zealous age was nonetheless laudable.

The use of rhymes by these early friars was undoubtedly a potent means of bringing the people closer to the spirit of the Church's liturgy, and in general of counteracting the influence of less edifying poems and ballads. The vernacular translations of Latin hymns by Friar William Herbert is a case in point.[48] Mr. Carleton Brown, editor of the hymns, sees in them "an early attempt on the part of the friars to introduce vernacular versions of the hymns into their preaching. There can be little question, I think, that these pieces were designed primarily for pulpit use."[49] They might also have served for congregational singing. Original verses in the vernacular of a still earlier composition can be traced to the pens of English Franciscans. The "Love Rune" of Friar

---

45. Margaret Deansley, *The Lollard Bible and Other Medieval Biblical Versions* (Cambridge, 1920), p. 148, note.

46. See Appendix II.

47. Owst, *op. cit.*, p. 82.

48. He died in 1333. *Dictionary of Nat. Biography,* XXVI, 218. See on his hymns "E. H. R.," 1934, pp. 299-302.

49. *Religious Lyrics of the Fourteenth Century* (Oxford, 1924), p. xiv. For an example of a rhymed sermon of the early fourteenth century, see Heuser, *Kildare-Gedichte* (Bonn, 1904), pp. 89-96.

Thomas of Hales "is one of the few English poems of the thirteenth century which was still remembered and imitated as late as the end of the fourteenth century."[50] "A Song of Sorrow for the Passion," "An Orison of Penitence to Our Lady" and "I Will Become a Friar" are among many others very likely of Franciscan composition. Still other poems and hymns were collected by the Franciscans.[51] Thus we have the English sons of St. Francis preparing the way for Chaucer in much the same way that St. Francis himself prepared the way for Dante. Both English and Italian owe much in their development to the friars. As to their influence on English prose, Dr. Little makes the following reflection: "It has often occasioned surprise that the generation which saw the rise of poetry in England, saw also the rise of English prose — that, in a word, Wyclif was the contemporary of Chaucer. When we remember that, for a century and a half, men versed in all the learning of their time had been constantly preaching to the people in the vulgar tongue in every part of the country, we shall see less cause to wonder at the vigorous language, the clear and direct expression, of 'the father of English prose.' "[52] Not even literature could escape the Franciscan effort to re-christianize society and save it from its sordid self.

It is somewhat strange that in the story of Franciscan influence in England little evidence is available regarding efforts to establish the Third Order or Tertiary fraternities there. In Italy,

---

50. Carleton Brown, ed., *English Lyrics of the Thirteenth Century* (Oxford, 1932), p. 198. Cf. also pp. 68-72. Thomas of Hales flourished about 1250 (*Dict. Nat. Biography,* XXIV, 36).

51. *English Lyrics of the Thirteenth Century,* pp. 122-24, 218; also pp. xx-xxii, xxxii-xxxiii. See Appendix IV for the Franciscan composition, "I Will Become a Friar."

52. A. G. Little, *Grey Friars in Oxford,* p. 64. One may very well accept Dr. Little's claim for the influence of the friars in the revival and development of English prose without accepting his implied acceptance of Wyclif as "the father of English prose." Modern scholarship would seem to have disposed of this long-held notion regarding Wyclif's place in the evolution of our language. See R. W. Chambers, *On the Continuity of English Prose from Alfred to More and His School,* an extract from the introduction to Nicholas Harpsfield's life of Sir Thomas More (Early English Text Society, London, 1932), especially pp. ci-cix.

and to some extent in Germany, these laymen and laywomen enrolled under the Franciscan banner proved a powerful force for putting down petty wars and in general raising the tone of social relations.[53] A list of Franciscan provinces and foundations of 1385 assigns four Tertiary congregations to England and three to Scotland,[54] but so far there appears to be no other information about them. It is possible that the list embraces such rather nebulous groups as the Franciscan Sisters whom we hear of at Northampton in 1252,[55] or at Belby in 1268,[56] or even the Sisters of St. Damian concerning whom Pope Innocent IV warned the English bishops in 1251 that they must not be allowed to build houses without the permission of the Provincial of the Friars Minor.[57]

There were also probably quite a few Tertiaries who did not belong to organized fraternities. These the friars would no doubt have encouraged, while they found Tertiary fraternities an unpleasant burden.[58] That the friars did enrol prominent lay people as Tertiaries cannot be doubted. Under the year 1296 the *Lanercost Chronicle* tells of a holy anchoress named Emma of Shrewsbury who wore the Franciscan habit and received the friars to

---

53. See Father Cuthbert, *Life of St. Francis,* pp. 283-90; *Bullarium Franciscanum,* I, 39-40, 71, 99, 108, 142-3, etc.; A. Koch, *Frueheste Niederlassungen der Minoriten im Rheingebiet,* pp. 14, 82-3, etc.; *Archivum Franciscanum historicum,* XIV, 138-98; 442-60; XV, 349-81; XVII, 237-381; XVIII, 63-89, etc.

54. Series *Provinciarum ragusina,* MS. Canonici Miscell. 525 (20001), fol. 241, in Bodleian Library, Oxford. See Dr. Little's critical treatment in *Opuscules de critique historique,* I, 251-97 (Paris, 1903), in which the list is printed (p. 296); or see Golubovich, *Biblioteca bio-bibliografica della Terra Santa,* II, 254-60.

55. A. F. C. Bourdillon, *The Order of Minoresses in England,* Brit. Soc. Fran. Studies, vol. XII, p. 11.

56. *Cal. Pat., 1266-1272,* p. 255.

57. *Register* of Archbishop Giffard, Surtees Soc., vol. 109, p. 93.

58. St. Bonaventure found it necessary (*Opera omnia,* VIII, pp. 368-9), to answer the question why the friars did not promote the Order of Penitents. He gave among other reasons, the following: 1) The friars will be expected to devote too much attention to these penitents; 2) They will be expected to intercede for them at court when the penitents are in difficulties; 3) The friars will be charged with their faults, debts, etc.

Individual Tertiaries, on the other hand, might prove to be influential friends or generous benefactors such as the *confratres* and *consorores* enrolled by the Letters of Fraternity. See below, p. 38, note 62.

hospitality.[59] Still earlier, in 1291, we have the story of how Sir Walter de Wyneborne urged Peter Quivil, Bishop of Exeter, to carry out the king's request that the Exeter Franciscans be given a more healthy site for their friary. The bishop had promised to fulfil the king's wish, but a Dominican adviser hostile to the Franciscans succeeded in dissuading him. When Sir Walter therefore pressed him, "the bishop answered him with a high spirit, 'Are you then a wearer of the Cord, and wish to drive me out of my own bishopric?' "[60] It is thus very likely that many of the friars' friends and benefactors were Cord-bearers or Tertiaries. This would help to explain, too, why so many prominent citizens sought burial in Franciscan churches.[61] On the other hand, there appears to be no evidence that the English Franciscans used Letters of Fraternity before the end of the fourteenth century.[62]

As to the Second Order, or Poor Clares, the first definite information we have of their establishing themselves in England comes from the Patent and Close Rolls of 1393-1394. We know of a house at London outside Aldgate, and another at Waterbeach, later transferred to Denny, but the movement never became widespread.[63] The papal bull, *Loca sanctorum,* which grants indulgences to those visiting the Church of the *Clarissas* outside the walls of London as early as 1281, is clearly misdated, and from available evidence we are forced to date the arrival of the first

---

59. P. 183.

60. *The Franciscans and Dominicans of Exeter* (Little and Easterling, Exeter, 1927), p. 16.

61. See chap. III.

62. See articles by Clark-Maxwell in *Archaeologia,* vol. 75, pp. 19-60 and vol. 79, pp. 179-216. These Letters of Fraternity first appeared among religious orders in the thirteenth century and later became prevalent among virtually all of them. By them benefactors were enrolled as *confratres* and *consorores* and became partakers in the spiritual works of the community to which they gave aid.

63. See Bourdillon, *Order of Minoresses in England,* pp. 13 *et seq.; Cal. Pat., 1292-1301,* p. 24; *Cal. Close, 1288-1296,* p. 442. The lists printed by Golubovich, *Biblioteca bio-bibliografica,* II, 249 *et seq.,* assign no less than twelve to twenty Poor Clare houses to fourteenth-century England. That of 1385 giving three houses is most in keeping with available records.

Poor Clares in England at 1293 or 1294.[64] Aside from the lively interest taken in these nuns by the king's brother, Edmund, his wife Blanche, Queen of Navarre, and others of the royal family, we know little about them. However the names, Minories and Clare Street, London, have not allowed their memory to die.[65]

When we turn to the friars' efforts to alleviate physical suffering and distress among their fellow-men, we are confronted by a scarcity of evidence. Nevertheless, however silent the records, tradition persists in giving us a friar devoted to the physical, as well as the spiritual, well-being of those who suffer and strive; a friar whose understanding and sympathy goes out to every form of ailment to which the soul and body of man are heirs. Shakespeare's Friar Lawrence,[66] who knows the medicinal qualities of herbs and the power of prayer, as well as the hearts of passionate young lovers; Manzoni's Fra Cristoforo,[67] who defends the poor and the humble against the rich and the proud, brings a wise and tactful intervention to bear upon the troubles of a home, a father's understanding to the difficulties of a man and his maid, a mother's self-sacrificing care to the victims of the plague — these are the types of Franciscan friar which endure in spite of the Wyclifs and the John Balls who would blacken their record. Even the degenerate friar of Chaucer's *Canterbury Tales,* who had come to know "the tavernes wel in every toun and everich hostiler and tappestere bet than a lazar or a beggestere," suggests the nobler reputation enjoyed by his predecessors; and he himself is still sympathetic and trusted enough to make "many a mariage of young wymmen, at

---

64. *Bullarium Fran.,* III, 471. The Poor Clares at Waterbeach received similar privileges at the same time. Wadding's date, 1292 (*Annales Minorum,* V, 309, ¶XLII), for the London foundation is also evidently wrong. In June, 1293, the nuns are still "being brought" (*Cal. Pat., 1292-1301,* p. 24), and in March, 1295, they are still a new order "that has arisen in this realm" (*Cal. Close, 1288-1296,* p. 442). The Waterbeach house began probably in 1294-5 (*Cal. Chancery Warrants, 1244-1326,* p. 40).

65. See *Royal Commission on Hist. Monuments,* V, 72a. For interest of the royal family, see *Cal. Pat., 1292-1301,* pp. 86, 105-6, 168, 170, 296, etc.

66. *Romeo and Juliet,* esp. Act. IV, Scene II.

67. *I Promessi Sposi.*

his own cost."[68] The English friars enjoyed the reputation of matchmakers from the earliest times;[69] and the good they accomplished thereby must not be overlooked and disparaged on account of such stories as the "Summoner's Tale" of Chaucer.

Writers of textbooks and general treatises on medieval English life often take it for granted that the first Franciscans nursed the lepers and the plague-stricken. Knowing their loyalty to the wish and example of St. Francis, one is inclined to believe that the friars lent a hand wherever required. Their aspiration was to help men to a better appreciation of the Incarnate God and His message of love for suffering humanity. When the consciousness of the dangers in their work for the salvation of souls troubled them, Bishop Grosseteste offered the consolation that their work was too important and necessary to be put aside on account of its dangers. One does not refuse to extinguish a conflagration, he reminded them, even though he be somewhat blackened by the smoke and flames. One must stoop down to raise another up; and "the Saviour will easily restore the ornament of a soul which has been soiled in His honor."[70]

Properly taken, this might be called a summary of the Franciscan philosophy of service. They must stoop down in order to save, and the risks involved to their own souls must be offset by prayer and self-denial. St. Francis had given an example of the proper balance between the contemplative and the active life. He, certainly, found spiritual consolation in the care of the poor and the physically afflicted. By an *a priori* judgment we might conclude that his zealous English followers aspired to the same end. But the Franciscan alleviation of suffering was primarily spiritual. It may have been a sort of Franciscan instinct which led the first English friars to seek temporary homes in hospitals,[71] as the Ger-

---

68. *Prologue.*

69. Matthew Paris, *Chron. maj.*, IV, 279. For instances of their acting as go-betweens among noble persons, see *ibid.*, III, 324 and this essay, chap. IV.

70. *Lanercost Chronicle*, p. 44.

71. Eccleston, pp. 8, 12, 13.

man friars also did;[72] and it may not be far-fetched to argue, with Dr. Karl Mueller, that they were hardly mere idle guests at these places.[73] Or, again, we might be led to find significance in the fact that Alexander, Master of the priests' hospital at Canterbury, eventually provided the friars with a plot of ground and a chapel;[74] that Thomas, Master of St. Peter's Hospital, York, joined the friars in 1270;[75] or that Bartholomew, Master of the Hospital of St. Bartholomew, London, and the brothers of this same institution were benefactors of the Franciscans in Stinking Lane.[76] Similarly, we might recall that in 1230 the Franciscans of Rochelle, France, then under the English, received from Henry III a confirmation of the rights of the lepers in St. Bartholomew's Hospital at Rochelle;[77] and that in 1290 John Pecham, Franciscan Archbishop of Canterbury, took charge of the church of Raculver so that its declining revenues might be increased for the benefit of the lepers of Herebaldon Hospital and the poor of Northgate Hospital.[78] But the fact still remains that no direct or conclusive evidence has so far appeared that the English Franciscans ever engaged in nursing the lepers or other unfortunates.

A cursory glance through the calendars of Patent, Close and Liberate Rolls reveals the fact that there were leper colonies or hospitals in at least eight towns where the Franciscans had friaries; that is, Oxford, Chester, Lichfield, Worcester, Coventry, Lincoln, York and London. There were probably many more such towns. But the very existence of these hospitals all over England helps to explain why the English friars did not turn to nursing as they did in Italy. There were some two hundred

---

72. *Chronica Jordani,* nos. 32 and 45.
73. *Die Anfaenge des Minoritenordens,* etc., p. 98.
74. Eccleston, p. 25.
75. *Register* of Archbishop Giffard, p. 257.
76. *Monumenta Franciscana,* I, 499.
77. *Patent Rolls, 1225-1232,* p. 393.
78. *Cal. Pat., 1281-1292,* pp. 361 and 410; also W. H. Bliss, ed., *Cal. of Papal Letters* (London, 1893-1897), vol. I, 511.

lazar houses in England in the course of the Middle Ages,[79] and English hospitals generally were well organized and provided for. Most of them were founded before the arrival of the friars. They were semi-independent institutions under royal and episcopal control, and it is doubtful if the friars would have been welcome as helpers in most of them.[80] At least there was not the desperate need for them there was in Italy.

There is some evidence to show that the English Franciscans came to the relief of distress in other ways than nursing lepers. Not to dwell on the miracles some of them are supposed to have wrought in favor of the afflicted,[81] there is the story from the *Lanercost Chronicle*[82] of the Franciscans who brought medicine to the dying prebendary of Wells whom they sought to care for in his illness. We know, too, that at least one of the early friars, Adam de Bechesoueres (or Hekeshove), was a famous physician.[83]

An entry in the Close Rolls for 1236 suggests another phase of the "social" activities of the medieval friars. It is an order from the king to the constable of the Tower of London to receive certain prisoners and to keep them so secluded that they cannot talk to each other "or with a Friar Preacher or Minor, or anyone of whatsoever religion."[84] This specific mention of the friars evokes a vision of what was probably part of their routine work, namely, visiting the imprisoned. The entry is the more significant when taken in connection with other records of similar import, for example, Matthew Paris' account of the friars' saving a number of Jews from death after they had been imprisoned for the

---

79. R. M. Clay, *The Medieval Hospitals of England,* p. 35.

80. *Ibid.,* p. 211.

81. E. g., see Paris' *Chron. maj.,* III, 312-13; Eccleston, p. 76, etc.

82. P. 153.

83. *Mon. Fran.,* I, 137 and 320, where Adam Marsh recommends his services to Bishop Grosseteste and John of Reading. See also pp. 333, 388-9, 404. Roger Bacon exhibited a remarkable knowledge of medicine and anatomy. Cf. Edward Lutz, O. F. M., *Roger Bacon's Contribution to Knowledge* (*Franciscan Studies,* XVII, St. Anthony Guild Press, Paterson, N. J., 1936), pp. 45 *et seq.* and references.

84. *Close Rolls, 1234-1237,* p. 363.

murder of a Christian lad, Hugh of Lincoln.[85] Paris is mildly scandalized at the friars' action, and the people for a time withdrew their alms, such was their anti-Jewish fanaticism, but even Paris is inclined to think that the motive of the liberators was a good one.[86] There were many other occasions when influential Franciscans came to the rescue of condemned persons. In 1258 the papal nuncio, Friar Mansuetus, obtained the pardon of men charged with murder.[87] William of Gainsborough frequently used his good offices in favor of accused people.[88] At one time an outlaw might be pardoned by the king at the instance of a friar,[89] at another a person might be freed from a charge of heresy on a friar's pledge.[90] In 1338 two Canterbury Franciscans, John atte Noke of Newington and John de Bromesdon, were pardoned by the king for rescuing certain felons who were on the way to execution after being sentenced to death by justices of the king's bench.[91]

In some of these and similar instances, personal considerations or other than purely charitable motives may have prompted the conduct of the friars, but the incidents do point to the influence of the Franciscans and the fact that they were ready to use it in the interest of unfortunates.

A model and fairly typical Franciscan was Adam Marsh, the great educator and scholar, friend and counselor of princes and prelates as well as of the humble and the poor. No one was above his advice and reproach, no one below his kindly interest and charity. Of his activities among the great ones of this world

---

85. *Chron. maj.*, V, p. 546.

86. *Ibid., loc. cit.* The *Lanercost Chronicle* credits the saving of the Jews specifically to Adam Marsh, who was so influential with the king. The Burton Annalist (*Annales monastici,* R. S., I, 346-7) attributes it to the Dominicans. Both orders may have been involved.

87. *Cal. Pat., 1247-1258,* p. 627.

88. *Cal. Pat., 1292-1301,* pp. 146, 256; *1301-1307,* p. 63; *Cal. Close, 1302-1307,* p. 18; compare *ibid.*, pp. 388, 392, 400, etc.

89. *Cal. Pat., 1232-1247,* p. 11.

90. *Close Rolls, 1237-1242,* p. 368.

91. *Cal. Pat., 1338-1340,* p. 19.

we shall hear more later. Here we are interested in him as the friend of the little ones. Amidst all the cares which weighed him down, his busy pen took up the cause, now of a woman who was pinched with poverty,[92] now of a poor woman oppressed in a matrimonial suit,[93] again of a widow beset by her enemies.[94] He penned letters in favor of a poor scholar in need of help,[95] an unfortunate monk who threw off his habit as a novice and later repented,[96] repentant and apostate friars,[97] a sick friar,[98] a nun,[99] a priest,[100] a rector,[101] a repentant thief,[102] a goldsmith,[103] and other unnamed persons.[104] Rightly does Professor Brewer observe that these letters not only illustrate the character of Friar Adam Marsh but "what, perhaps, is of no less importance, the character of the order to which he belonged. For this assiduity was not singular; it was exemplified in others more celebrated than Adam de Marisco for their scholastic attainments; and it helps us to understand the immense influence enjoyed by the friars in their better days."[105]

John Pecham was such another friar. A great scholar of both Oxford and Paris and lecturer to the cardinals of the Papal Curia, he was later (1278-1292) made Archbishop of Canterbury, the primal see of England.[106] The cares of his office were many and arduous, yet his letters, like those of Adam Marsh, show how

---

92. *Monumenta Franciscana,* I., 205.
93. *Ibid.,* p. 260.
94. *Ibid.,* p. 398.
95. *Ibid.,* p. 244.
96. *Ibid.,* p. 177.
97. *Ibid.,* pp. 351, 361, 374.
98. *Ibid.,* pp. 304, 334.
99. *Ibid.,* pp. 164, 239.
100. *Ibid.,* p. 240.
101. *Ibid.,* p. 399.
102. *Ibid.,* p. 340.
103. *Ibid.,* p. 240.
104. *Ibid.,* pp. 220, 260. See also pp. 396, 397, 399, 404, 405, etc.
105. *Ibid.,* p. lxxxv.
106. Little, *Grey Friars in Oxford,* pp. 154-6; *Mon. Fran.,* I, 552; *Lanercost Chronicle,* pp. 100, 101; *Dictionary of National Biography.*

close to his heart were the poor and the suffering. We have already mentioned his recall of the Raculver church the better to provide for lepers and the poor.[107] More striking instances of his spirit are not far to seek. To the Bishop of Lichfield and Coventry he wrote in his candid manner: "We simply forbid you, your officials and all your ministers to make any pecuniary exactions or collections except in that case and form in which they are permitted by canonical sanctions." Instead of practising oppression, the bishop and his ministers are to distribute intestate property to the poor, abolish abuses and see to it that uniformity is observed in the collection of tithes.[108] Similarly, he wrote to the Bishop of Norwich to stop the extortions being practised by the bishop's officials.[109] Nor did he spare his own officials, but wrote to the Prior of Yarmouth for evidence regarding the alleged exactions being practised by his own clerks against his will and command.[110] Again, he directed that the farm of a certain church be given to the poor;[111] ordered the release of persons unjustly imprisoned;[112] pleaded for a woman who had been wronged by her husband.[113] Many more instances might be added, but enough have been adduced to explain the following tribute to the great friar and archbishop by Mr. Martin, editor of his letters: "In forming an estimate of Pecham's character, his frequent exertions in favor of the poor, and against anything like oppression, must not be overlooked. The persons and the causes are very various. Now he rebukes a noble landowner for keeping too large a head of game, now he threatens a bishop for allowing his officials to sequester benefices and extort money for releasing them; and shows equal willingness to stop similar practices of which his

---

107. This chapter, p. 41.
108. *Register epistolarum,* R. S., pp. 167-8.
109. *Ibid.,* p. 177.
110. *Ibid.,* pp. 176-7.
111. *Ibid.,* p. 194.
112. *Ibid.,* pp. 373-5.
113. *Ibid.,* pp. 387-8.

own clerks are accused. He asserts the rights of his tenants to the ferry of Lambeth against the Abbot of Westminster, attempts to help a poor man who had mortgaged land to a convent, and in many other ways shows the sympathy for the poor which he had learnt as a friar."[114]

If further proof were needed of the early English Franciscans' devotion to the poor, we might instance Friar John of Wales' instructions to preachers,[115] or the fact that in 1291 Gregory de Rokesley, Mayor of London, left the residue of his estate in the dioceses of London, Canterbury and Rochester to the poor, and instructed his executors to consult the wardens of the Friars Minor in London and Canterbury about its disposal.[116] The friars, it was presumed, could best be trusted to give the proper counsel when there was a question of helping those whose interests they had so much at heart. This Franciscan virtue is well brought out by Matthew Paris' account of how the friars dared even to offend their great benefactor and protector, the king, rather than condone injustice to the poor. The king had sent the friars a cartload of wool cloth for habits as an alms. Hearing, however, that the cloth had been confiscated from some merchants, the friars sent the whole load back to the king with the explanation that it was not lawful to bestow alms out of the spoliation of the poor, and they would never be the recipients of such a gift. Even Matthew Paris was satisfied that this action redounded to the friars' credit.[117]

For the rest, even had the sixteenth-century reformers been less thorough in their work of destruction, we could hardly expect to find extensive records of the work of the friars among the poor and the outcast, the flotsam and jetsam of humanity. They were too busy with their work to concern themselves with

114. *Ibid.*, p. lxxiii.

115. See chap. III, pp. 48, 49.

116. From the *Calendar of Wills of the Court of Hustings*, I, 99, referred to in *Victoria County Histories*, Kent, II, 191.

117. *Chron. maj.*, V, 275-6.

recording their routine deeds for posterity. We have witnessed some, and shall witness more, of the spirit which actuated them. Deeds must of necessity have followed. But there is nothing to be gained by trying to "make a case" for what today would be termed social work. If the friars had done nothing more than bring to the impoverished and illiterate masses the consolations of religion, they could still be reckoned among the greatest social workers of all time. It is significant that one who has had much experience as a social worker in the slums of a great modern metropolis should plead for religion as the prime necessity for social uplift among the teeming millions who dwell there, and long for the return of the wandering friar as the solution to our greatest modern social problem.[118]

---

118. Alexander Paterson, *Across the Bridges* (London, 1911), pp. 253-4. It is interesting to speculate on the influence exerted by the Franciscans and Dominicans on the origin and spread of other orders of friars and congregations of religious-minded people who set out to correct the evils of their day. If, as Salimbene admitted ("Chronica," *Mon. Germ. Hist.*, XXXII, 254), "we and the Friars Preachers have taught all men to beg," it is also true that they taught them many nobler things. The Brothers of the Penance of Jesus Christ (or Friars of the Sack as they were called) were founded by a former Franciscan novice in Provence (Salimbene, *op. cit.*, pp. 254-5), and the Franciscans gave them, as well as the Augustinians and Carmelites, hospitality and encouragement when they came to England (Eccleston, pp. 129-31 and notes).

III

THE FRIARS AND THE NOBILITY

Though extremely popular, the Franciscan movement was clearly not "proletarian." St. Francis and many of his first companions, such as Bernard of Quintavalle, Peter Cataneo, Angelo Tancredi, and Sylvester and Leo were from the class of well-to-do burghers, lesser nobility and clerics. And the movement was not so much toward economic betterment as toward spiritual uplift. It was a revolt against the luxury, greed and general worldliness of the social, economic, cultural and religious life of the age.[1] In this the Franciscans had much in common with the Humiliati and Waldenses who preceded them.[2] But, while the earlier movements, lacking the approval of the Church, drifted toward heresy and the violent overthrow of both authority and doctrine, the Franciscans, with ecclesiastical approval, set out to effect reforms within the existing framework of society and the Church. They preached evangelical living chiefly by their own lives. Content with the rudest and simplest in clothing, fare and dwellings, they were nevertheless "not to despise or judge men whom they see clothed in fine and showy garments, using dainty meats and drinks."[3] However much their democratic spirit may have contributed to the ultimate downfall of the feudal system, the friars were not interested in systems as such, but in the saving of souls, of whatever class or occupation.

The *Summa collationum* of Friar John of Wales may be taken as a summary of the Franciscan attitude toward society.

---

1. H. Grundmann, *Religioese Bewegungen im Mittelalter* (*Historische Studien,* Heft 267) (Berlin, 1935), pp. 164 *et seq.*
2. *Ibid.,* pp. 157 *et seq.*
3. Franciscan Rule, chap. II. Cf. Paschal Robinson, *Writings of St. Francis of Assisi* (Philadelphia, 1906), p. 66.

In it Friar John lays down the rules which should govern the preacher of the Gospel in his dealing with all manner of men. All classes and conditions of men are good. It is the preacher's task to admonish and instruct everyone according to his needs and status, not to arouse discontent with one's lot.[4] The rich must not acquire their riches unjustly nor love them inordinately. Riches are a trust from God and should be used to help those in want and thus to purchase eternal riches in heaven.[5] Voluntary poverty is pleasing to God. The poor should be urged to bear their lot patiently and seek rather for spiritual riches.[6] Similarly, princes, judges, governors, soldiers, officials of the State and Church, laborers and the rest have their rights and duties, and each must be admonished and corrected accordingly.[7] Far from advocating class warfare, the Franciscans were a bond of unity between the various elements in society,[8] and it is this universal appeal which accounts for their favorable reception at the hands of prince and peasant alike in all the countries in which they settled.

If their first experiences with the English nobility were not very encouraging,[9] the difficulties were owing to misunderstanding and were only temporary. When these strangely-clad, barefoot enthusiasts became better known, the ruling classes rallied to their support. This, as already pointed out,[10] was due in the first instance largely to the friendly Loretta, Countess of Leicester, "who cherished the friars in all things as a mother cherishes her sons, discreetly winning for them the favor of princes and prelates, whose good-will she enjoyed to a remarkable degree."[11] At

4. *Summa collationum* (Paris, 1516), Prologue, fol. i.
5. *Ibid.,* Pars Tertia, Dist. IV, Cap. I.
6. *Ibid., loc. cit.,* Cap. II.
7. *Ibid., passim.*
8. See this essay, chap. IV and *passim.*
9. See chap. I, pp. 7-9.
10. Chap. I, p. 16.
11. Eccleston, pp. 25-6.

Canterbury, the friendship of Simon Langton and Henry of Sandwich may have been the result of Loretta's efforts.[12]

In London, the first friars also received important help from members of the lesser nobility. Some of their greatest benefactors were mayors, aldermen, sheriffs and other notable citizens.[13] In 1260-1261, Lady Ela, Countess of Warwick, extended the property the friars had acquired in Stinking Lane;[14] and John of Colchester, former almoner of Henry III,[15] Dionisia de Monte Caniso and others added to their property in the parish of St. Nicholas.[16] John of Brittany, Earl of Richmond; his niece, Mary, Countess of Pembroke; Robert de Lisle, first Baron de Rougemont; Gilbert de Clare, ninth Earl of Gloucester; his three sisters, Margaret, Countess of Gloucester, Eleanor, wife of Hugh the Despenser and Elizabeth, wife of John de Burgh, Earl of Ulster — these were some of the prominent benefactors of the famous Grey Friars' Church which was begun in the early fourteenth century.[17] The list of prominent persons buried there is even more imposing.[18]

What was taking place in London was taking place to a lesser degree in other parts of the kingdom. The knight, Richard Gobiun, gave the friars their first dwelling in Northampton; but when his son John became enamored of the friars and insisted on joining the community, Richard became angry and ordered the brethren to leave. "The friars thereupon prepared to go, while the lord stood outside the door awaiting their departure. They came two-by-two in procession, a feeble old brother with a psalter bringing up the rear. Seeing their simplicity and humility, and

---

12. *Ibid.*, p. 25.

13. See C. L. Kingsford, "Prima fundatio Fratrum Minorum Londoniae," *Mon. Fran.*, I, 493 *et seq.; The Grey Friars of London,* pp. 17, 18, 30 *et seq.*, 146 *et seq;* Eccleston, pp. 13, 19, 26-7, 158 *et seq.*

14. Kingsford, *op. cit.*, pp. 30, 150.

15. *Cal. Pat., 1272-1281,* p. 281.

16. *Cal. Pat., 1317-1321,* pp. 599, 600.

17. *Mon. Fran.*, I, 513-15; Kingsford, *op. cit.*, pp. 163 *et seq.*

18. E. B. S. Shepherd in the *Archaeological Journal,* LIX, 238-87; also Kingsford, *op. cit.*, pp. 70 *et seq.*

moved to compassion by divine inspiration, Richard broke into tears, insistently and devoutly crying and pleading that they would spare him and return. The brethren did so, and from that time he was like a father to them."[19]

Ralph Fitz-Randal, Lord of Middleham, was considered the founder of the Richmond friary, and his heart was buried in the choir of the church in 1270.[20] John of Brittany, Earl of Richmond, left a bequest to the friars there in 1304.[21] The Coventry friary was built on the estate of Ralph Blundeville, Earl of Chester.[22] Henry de Lacy, third Earl of Lincoln, was one of the benefactors of the York friary.[23] Edmund, Earl of Lancaster and younger son of Henry III, was a benefactor of the friary at Preston.[24] William Beauchamp, fifth Baron of Elmley, and the knight Sir Nicholas de Muthon were benefactors of the Worcester friars. William directed in his will that his body be buried in the friars' church, and Nicholas left his heart to be placed there. William's wife Maud and his son William, first Earl of Warwick and also a benefactor, were among the other notables buried in the Worcester church.[25] Richard, Earl of Cornwall and King of the Romans, was looked upon as the founder of the Franciscan church at Oxford. His heart was buried there, as well as the body of his third wife, Beatrice Falkenstein, and other prominent persons.[26] John Warenne, Earl of Surrey (died 1304), was a benefactor of the friaries at Lewes and Grantham.[27] His annuity to the Grantham friars was confirmed by his grandson and heir, also

19. Eccleston, pp. 29, 30.
20. *Victoria County Histories,* Yorks., III, 273.
21. *Ibid., loc. cit.*
22. *Victoria County Histories,* Warwicks., II, 103.
23. *Ibid.,* Yorks., III, 290.
24. *Ibid.,* Lancasters., II, 162.
25. *Ibid.,* Worcesters., II, 170-71. The monastic annalist of Worcester attributes William's decision to be buried with the friars to the influence of the Franciscan John Olney, who attended the baron on his deathbed (*Annales monastici,* R. S., IV, 537).
26. *Grey Friars in Oxford,* p. 25.
27. *Cal. Close, 1302-1307,* p. 246; *Cal. Pat., 1317-1321,* p. 66.

John Warenne, who himself assisted the friars.[28] Eleanor, Countess of Leicester, befriended the Leicester friars.[29] Richard, Earl of Gloucester, and Gilbert de Preston, justiciar of Henry III, befriended the friars of St. Edmund's Bury.[30] And so the list might be extended.

More important is the fact that members of the ruling classes joined the ranks of the friars. John Gobiun, mentioned above, was not an exception. Joyce of Cornhill, one of the first to enter the order in London, was the son of an alderman and sheriff.[31] Eccleston tells us that "many honest bachelors and many nobles" joined the friars at Oxford,[32] and enumerates some of the scholars and knights who brought prestige to the English Franciscans.[33] The king himself must have been impressed by the type of members the friars were able to attract when, on their reception of four knights, he remarked that with proper discretion in the reception of candidates they might rule over princes.[34] *The First Foundation of the Friars Minor of London*[35] gives a list of eminent persons who became Franciscans in England. Among them are such names as Robert Fitz-Walter, Baron and founder of the Colchester convent; Baron Robert de Lisle, benefactor of the London friars, who joined the order after the death of his wife;[36] Robert Hylton, Baron of Hylton; William Scharshill, former justiciar of Edward III; Ralph of Maidstone, former Bishop of Hereford; and John of Reading, former Abbot of Osney.[37]

The fact that members of noble families supported the Franciscans and joined their ranks does not in itself display the rela-

---

28. *Cal. Pat., 1317-1321,* p. 66, and *1334-1338,* p. 117.
29. *Close Rolls, 1253-1254,* p. 244.
30. *Memorials of St. Edmund's Abbey,* R. S., II, 267; Matthew Paris, *Chron. maj.,* V, 688.
31. Eccleston, pp. 19, 26; Kingsford, *op. cit.,* p. 147.
32. Eccleston, p. 27.
33. *Ibid.,* pp. 20-24.
34. *Ibid.,* p. 24; see this essay chap. I, p. 20.
35. *Mon. Fran.,* I, 541-42.
36. G. E. C., *Complete Peerage,* new edn., VIII, 73.
37. Robert Lamborn, Franciscan confessor to Queen Isabella, is also listed as a baron's son, but the claim is denied by Kingsford (*op. cit.,* p. 75).

tions between them in their true light. It does not explain the motives which actuated either of the parties. Even the worst behaved in a society which cherished a living faith in the supernatural might consider it a good investment to procure the prayers of holy men at the price of a few material goods. Or a disillusioned devotee of the world might well seek refuge in a monastery in order to devote his declining years to the salvation of his soul. John Warenne, Earl of Surrey and Sussex, for example, might ease his conscience and make some atonement for a reckless life by the surrender of a little of the wealth which in any case he could not take with him beyond the grave. Or Baron Robert de Lisle might find comfort in a religious house after his wife had died and he was advancing in years, just as the discredited Queen Isabella found refuge with the Minoresses.[38]

The Franciscans, however, were not merely contemplatives and ascetics. They were men of action intent upon serving and improving their fellow-men. And it was during the period of their greatest activity that, as Matthew Paris notes,[39] the nobles, clerics and prelates flocked to them. Furthermore, the friars, as Paris also notes,[40] were advisers to the "great ones" as well as preachers to the people, though he jealously questions the motives of the friars and charges them with extorting wills from the dying and lying in wait for the rich.[41] A satirical poem of the time of Edward I maintained that the Franciscans in their travels "take up their lodgings with the chief baron or knight, or with the chief person or priest, there where they can be satiated."[42] It is easy to impute motives. St. Bonaventure gave three reasons

---

38. See this chap., pp. 51 and 52 and chap. IV, pp. 94 and 95.

39. *Hist. Anglorum,* II, 298. The friars "officio praedicationis, studii et eruditionis strenue intenderunt, et ad eorum Ordinem nobiles, clerici et etiam praelati coeperunt convolare."

40. *Chron. maj.,* III, 332-34, 627; compare Koch, *Die fruehesten Niederlassungen* etc., pp. 74-5.

41. *Chron. maj.,* IV, p. 279.

42. Thomas Wright, ed., *The Order of Fair-Ease, Political Songs of England* (Camden Soc., 1839), VI, 145.

for this practice of the friars: (1) the necessity on their part of going, when tired out and hungry, where they could hope for refreshment; (2) consideration for the poor, who would lavish hospitality on them beyond what they could really afford; (3) the good of the rich, who especially need the example and guidance of the friars.[43] This is in keeping with Friar John of Wales' instruction to the preacher of the Gospel that he must make use even of the conversation at table to deliver his message, "so that he may dispense the food of life to those who minister food for the body."[44]

Certainly, the friars had something to offer which made them always welcome in the homes of the well-to-do. It has been suggested, and not without reason, that their good-fellowship and genius for story-telling made their presence desired.[45] Their learning and travel, their broad experience with men and affairs, and the great fund of anecdotes which made their preaching interesting would make their conversation equally interesting. But these things were only means to an end. The friars had as a prime objective the good of souls, and all things were grist for their mill. When we find them associated with families of the nobility, it is usually in the capacity of confessor and adviser. Even the notorious John Warenne had a Franciscan confessor toward the end of his life.[46] William de Valence, titular Earl of Pembroke, obtained papal permission in 1255 for the Franciscan Peter de Rupe to act as confessor to himself, his wife, children and household.[47] Friar Geoffrey de Aylesham was confessor to

---

43. *Opera omnia,* VIII, 352, 353. See *ibid.,* p. 353, the saint's four reasons why religious honor the rich more than the poor; briefly: 1) God has placed them over the poor in *mundi gloriam;* 2) The infirmity of the rich, who require this exterior deference; 3) More good comes of correcting a rich and powerful person; 4) They contribute more to the support of the friars and have more perplexities and pitfalls than the poor.

44. *Summa collationum,* Prologue.

45. *Grey Friars in Oxford,* pp. 6, 7.

46. *Dictionary of National Biography,* XX, 828.

47. *Cal. Papal Letters,* I, 321.

Gilbert, Earl of Gloucester.[48] William of Gainsborough was confessor to Isabella de Fortibus, Countess of Aumale and Devon and Lady of the Isle of Wight; and he ministered to her on her deathbed.[49] John of Brittany, Earl of Richmond (1266-1333/4), had Franciscans in his household;[50] and after he was taken prisoner by the Scots in the battle of Byland Abbey in 1322, King Edward sent Robert Staindrop, guardian of the York friary, "together with another English brother of the same order to stay with the earl if he wishes, for his recreation and solace."[51] John was eventually buried in the Franciscan church of Nantes.[52] Henry de Lacy, Earl of Lincoln (1249-1311), had a papal privilege to be accompanied by his Franciscan confessor, Michael of Merton.[53] When the earl was preparing for his expedition against the Scots in 1300, Archbishop Corbridge authorized Friar Michael and his *confrère,* Reginald of Kington, to act as confessors to the earl's troops from the York diocese.[54] There are other instances on record of Franciscans being authorized to hear the confessions of prominent persons.[55]

Naturally it is impossible, for the most part, to appraise the influence wielded by friar confessors among the ruling classes. It must be presumed that in general they used their positions to inculcate the high religious principles for which the Franciscan movement stood, even if external results — as in the case of Queen Isabella — did not always measure up to the ideal. Nor is it necessarily to the discredit of the friars that they encouraged their

48. *Mon. Fran.,* I, 514.

49. *Chronica maiorum et vicecomitum Londoniarum,* Camden Soc., vol. 34, p. cx; Henry Cole, ed., *Documents Illustrative of English History in the Thirteenth and Fourteenth Centuries* (London, 1844), p. 22.

50. *Cal. Pat., 1324-1327,* pp. 57-8.

51. *Ibid., 1321-1324,* p. 210.

52. *Complete Peerage* (1895 edn.), VI, 353.

53. *Cal. Papal Letters,* II, 7.

54. *Register* of Thomas Corbridge, Surtees Soc., vol. 38, pp. 23-4; also *Hist. Papers and Letters from the Northern Registers,* p. 143.

55. See, e. g., *Registers* of John de Sandale and Rigaud de Asserio, Bishops of Winchester, 1316-1323 (Hampshire Record Soc., 1893), pp. 508, 509; Kingsford, *Grey Friars of London,* p. 203.

penitents at times to contribute to the expansion and endowment of their work. Though it is possible to assign a purely selfish motive to Friar Geoffrey's persuasion of the Earl of Gloucester to contribute money and timber toward Grey Friars' Church, London,[56] the cause was certainly a worthy one and the earl could afford to make some recognition to the friars for their services. Certainly, no suspicious or ulterior motives should be ascribed to the Franciscan confessors of Mary St. Pol, Countess of Pembroke, and Lady Devorguilla, widow of Sir John Balliol. Mary's confessor is credited with influencing her establishment of Pembroke College, Cambridge, as well as a similar hall for poor students in Paris.[57] She certainly had Franciscans dwelling on her estate at Denny,[58] and established a convent there for the Poor Clares or Minoresses.[59] Friar Richard Slickburn, confessor to Lady Devorguilla, undoubtedly had much to do with her completion of Balliol College, Oxford, which was begun by her husband as a foundation for poor students, and left incomplete at his death in 1269.[60] In 1282 Devorguilla addressed the statutes of the new college to the Franciscan, Hugh of Hertepole, and Master William de Menyl; and two years later had Friar Richard act as her agent in the work of establishment.[61] In 1285 Richard was occupied with recovering money assigned to the college from Balliol's debtors;[62] and in 1287 he still had a decisive voice in the application of the money.[63] Franciscans continued to act as proctors or supervisors of the college, probably down to the Dissolution.[64]

---

56. *Mon. Fran.*, I, 514.
57. Kingsford, *Grey Friars of London,* p. 163; Parkinson, *Collectanea Anglo-Minoritica* (London, 1726), p. 78.
58. *Cal. Pat., 1324-1327,* p. 18.
59. A. F. C. Bourdillon, *The Order of Minoresses in England,* B. S. F. S., vol. XII, p. 18.
60. Little, *Grey Friars in Oxford,* pp. 9, 10.
61. H. E. Salter, ed., *The Oxford Deeds of Balliol College* (Oxford, 1913), pp. 277-80.
62. *Ibid.,* p. 331.
63. *Ibid.,* pp. 283-84.
64. Little, *op. cit.,* p. 10. Devorguilla also took a great interest in the Scottish Franciscans, and founded their houses at Dumfries and Dundee; M. Bryce, *The Scottish Grey Friars,* p. 19.

One of the best illustrations of the kind of influence exerted by Franciscans on the English governing classes is furnished by records from the time of Henry III's conflict with his barons. Here we find the Franciscan Adam Marsh and some of his *confrères* arraigned with Bishop Grosseteste and Simon de Montfort against arbitrary and inefficient rule and the rapacity of Henry's favorites. Grosseteste's attitude is well known. He favored the cause of the barons because he recognized in them the only hope of effecting much-needed reforms in the English Church and State.[65] Adam Marsh shared the bishop's viewpoint, and together they exerted their influence on Simon, leader of the barons.

About 1250 we find Adam writing to Grosseteste: "I return your lordship the sketch which you have written on the reign of despotism and tyranny[66] as you have sent it, signed with the seal of the Earl of Leicester. ... The earl has spoken to me about the salutary and magnificent proposition for liberating souls which heaven has put into your heart; he extols and praises it to an incredible degree, and embraces it with his noble zeal, and is ready to execute it as heaven may inspire, with the aid of helpers if he can find them. But being much concerned about your health, he insists that you should not personally undertake such a dangerous and difficult task."[67] Adam then goes on to assure the bishop that God often uses the weak to confound the strong, and that there are still those who have not bent the knee to Baal.

To Master Ralph of Canterbury Adam wrote about the same time: "As the noble Lord Simon, Earl of Leicester, who burns with a great desire both for the honor of God and the public good (on which desire for reasons both apparent and secret, the salvation of many is known to depend), ardently wishes the help of your presence, ... I appeal to your sweet zeal that you go to the earl without delay."[68] To the earl himself Adam offered

65. See Stevenson, *Robert Grosseteste,* pp. 219-22.
66. "De principatu regni et tyrannidis."
67. *Mon. Fran.,* I, 110, 111.
68. *Ibid.,* pp. 225-26.

encouragement by reminding him of the reward he might one day expect for his indefatigable efforts to "purge, illuminate and sanctify the Church by a fitting government."[69] Later he urges the earl to trust in God for a favorable outcome to certain affairs of which Simon had written, for even though there is little hope for such circumspect counsel as the business requires, there must be no doubting the Divine Goodness in Whose keeping are the hearts of kings.[70] Adam had spoken to the king and queen in the earl's behalf,[71] and found them, together with the archbishop and others, more favorably inclined toward Simon.[72]

The tireless friar became anxious about this "necessary work of salvation in the kingdom of England, the delay of which is sure to be attended with the greatest dangers," and he cautioned the earl to be very circumspect in speaking of the affair. He himself had lately incurred the anger of the king and banishment from the royal presence for speaking too plainly. The friar was pleased to learn that his *confrère,* Gregory de Bosellis, had come to visit the earl in Gascony, and felt sure that Gregory would be helpful to both the earl and his countess.[73] Adam was disappointed that he had been prevented from seeing them, and he must not entrust to writing what he had to communicate. "Touching the affair of which you know, I think I ought to write nothing this time, especially as an important matter is at stake, which gives rise on one hand to the hope of the greatest salvation, and on the other fears of the greatest dangers." The lifeless written word, continued the friar, is after all an inadequate medium in such an important matter as this, and there is always the danger of

69. *Ibid.,* p. 264.

70. *Ibid.,* p. 265.

71. *Ibid.,* p. 268.

72. *Ibid.,* p. 281. This and the two immediately preceding references probably relate to the difficulties and misunderstandings which arose out of Simon's Gasconian campaign fought in Henry's interest; but the earl's ability to effect reforms in England would also depend on his success in France and the prestige and good-will he might win thereby in England.

73. *Ibid.,* pp. 270-76.

betrayal, by which salutary causes might suffer irreparable harm. The earl must not be displeased with his silence. The Bishops of Lincoln and Worcester, and Friar Gregory, then with the earl, would be able to counsel him better in matters which could not be deferred.[74]

Adam's letters to Bishop Grosseteste are equally mysterious. The leaders of the army of Christ are giving way before their enemies. Evil days are come, and Adam would like to speak to his lordship on what to do. He has spoken to the king and his counselors as they passed through Oxford bearing some fictitious charges already known to the bishop. But God will assist him who stands firm in defense of the truth. The king would be favorable enough were it not for his evil advisers.[75] Again, Adam sees an improvement in the situation in England, but he will not rest satisfied until the bishop's cause has succeeded.[76]

What this great cause might be we are not told. Was it the cause for which Simon de Montfort later fought at Lewes and Evesham? Essentially, such it was undoubtedly. The reforms demanded by the Oxford Provisions, the demands made by Simon on the eve of the battle of Lewes, and finally the provisions of the Mise of Lewes all coincide in general with the reforms demanded by Grosseteste in the parliament of 1244 and again in 1252.[77] It was a struggle involving both constitutional and ecclesiastical liberties, virtually the same principles which were at stake at 1233 when Grosseteste befriended the rebellious Richard Marshal, Earl of Pembroke,[78] and the friars pleaded with the king

74. *Ibid.*, pp. 276-78.
75. *Ibid.*, pp. 141-42.
76. *Ibid.*, p. 163.
77. Namely, in general, reforms in state and ecclesiastical administration by the curbing of alien favorites and benefice-holders; justices of the peace; elected representatives from the counties; and a body of native councilors to supervise the king's acts in the public interest. See especially C. Bémont, *Simon de Montfort*, trans. by E. F. Jacob (Oxford, 1930), pp. 215-20; *Chronicle of Gervase of Canterbury* (Continuator), R. S., II, 236; F. S. Stevenson, *Robert Grosseteste*, pp. 219-22, 302-5.
78. *Robert Grosseteste*, pp. 93-4; Bémont, *op. cit.*, p. 58; *R. Grosseteste epistolae*, R. S., pp. 38-43.

to show greater love toward his subjects.[79] Because the country was badly governed, Grosseteste was driven to take drastic action on his own. The friars gave him support and were even blamed for instigating measures to which the king took exception.[80] The bishop's was an ungrateful task, and there were too few who sympathized with his ideas and efforts. That is why he loved so much the friars who coöperated with him. And that, too, is probably why he recommended that Archbishop Boniface, who was too prone to play into the hands of Henry and his party, "should have continually at his side such assistance as could nowhere else be found except with the friars of both orders."[81] Though Grosseteste later had other Franciscans about him and protested that he loved them above all others and found them his most efficient helpers in the apostolate,[82] he could at one time write to Adam Marsh: "I have found in you, and in you alone, a truthful friend, a faithful counselor."[83]

But neither Grosseteste nor the Franciscans were for violent measures.[84] They sought to effect as far as might be by peaceful means the reforms which Simon and his party, after the death of Grosseteste and Adam Marsh, sought to effect by the sword. Reinhold Pauli is undoubtedly correct when he writes of Simon and his wife Eleanor that "it was part of the destiny of their lives that, living in familiar intercourse with the band of Minorites, who were struggling against the deep moral corruption of the time, they both saw the duties of the king and bishops and nobles in a totally different light from that in which they appeared for the most part to those dignitaries themselves. The Franciscan doctrine of lowliness and humility opened their hearts to sympathize with the common people, and they, in short, attained views

79. Paris., *Chron. maj.*, III, 251.
80. *Ibid.*, IV, 579-80; *Robert Grosseteste*, pp. 266-7.
81. *R. Grosseteste epistolae*, p. 336.
82. *Ibid.*, pp. 133-4.
83. *Ibid.*, p. 69.
84. *Robert Grosseteste*, p. 337. Reinhold Pauli, *Simon de Montfort, Earl of Leicester*, trans. by E. M. Goodwin (London, 1876), p. 73.

in life very rare for their time and station. The family was inspired by peculiar religious and political convictions."[85] And Dr. Pauli is likewise correct in pointing out that the Franciscans had much to do with preparing the people for constitutional government and formulating "so strikingly the demands of the barons and burghers, the supremacy of law over arbitrary will."[86] Contemporary literature gives abundant evidence of the popularity of the baronial cause;[87] and Mr. Treharne points out that the barons were anxious to right the wrongs also of the lesser freemen, and that their petition was neither a class document nor an indefinite reform proposal.[88] Nevertheless, however well all this may have fitted into the Franciscan view of things, the friars loved peace and it is unlikely that they would have encouraged war as a means of attaining the reforms demanded.

In the first place, we know that in the case of Richard Marshal, Blessed Agnellus of Pisa spent himself in the interests of peace.[89] Before and after the battle of Lewes, Franciscans were again occupied as peacemakers.[90] But in both cases there were personal grievances, passion and broken promises to contend with; and in the case of Simon, death had deprived him of the powerful directing influence of Bishop Grosseteste and Adam Marsh. "The only wholesome check upon Simon's ambition and self-confidence, perhaps [also upon] their common desire [Simon's and Eleanor's] to retaliate upon their enemies, was thus removed. Though the noble convictions and principles which they had derived from that connection remained unchanged, it certainly was not an accident that now, when Leicester was fifty years of age,

---

85. *Simon de Montfort, Earl of Leicester,* p. 87.
86. Pauli, *Bilder aus Alt-England* (London, 1860), p. 58.
87. *Political Songs of England,* Camden Soc., vol. VI, p. x.
88. Treharne, *The Baronial Plan of Reform* (Manchester, 1932), p. 71.
89. See this essay, chap. VI, pp. 166-68.
90. *Chronicle of Gervase of Canterbury,* II, 236; Walsingham, *Ypodigma Neustriae,* R. S., pp. 154-5; Rishanger, *Chronica et annales,* R. S., p. 28; *Chronicon Henrici Knighton,* R. S., I, 249; Walter de Heminburgh, *Chronicon,* edited by H. C. Hamilton (London, 1848), II, 318.

and had outgrown priestly advice, he entered upon a new course of public life, where he was no longer protected against arrogance and other obvious perils."[91]

It is not that the Franciscans were no longer associated with Simon and his wife, or that Adam Marsh was the only friar in whom they confided. Friar Gregory de Bosellis was a close friend of both Simon and Eleanor.[92] Others, as noted above, were with him before and after Lewes, and were likely members of his household.[93] But, supposing that Gregory was still alive or that the others were really close to the earl, it is unlikely that any of them could command the same respect as Adam Marsh. Adam knew both the weakness and the strength of Simon and Eleanor, was familiar with the most intimate affairs of their lives and household. He reported Eleanor's condition to the absent earl,[94] congratulated the countess on the birth of her child,[95] concerned himself with the education of their children.[96] He knew when to praise and encourage, when to admonish and warn, when to administer a rebuke. Thus, in the same letter that he gave Simon news of Eleanor, he rebuked the earl for presuming to take along with him to Gascony the parish priest of Hodiham without regard to the souls of the people and the law of the Church.[97] Again, he praised the earl for his zeal in the service of the Church, but reminded him that patience and self-conquest are better than the conquest of a city.[98] The friar was even more frank with the countess: lecturing her on her duties as wife and cautioning her against anger and extravagance in dress,[99] pointing out her ob-

---

91. Reinhold Pauli, *Simon de Montfort,* pp. 87-8.
92. *Mon. Fran.,* I, 277-78, 281, 292-3, 368.
93. C. L. Kingsford, ed., *The Song of Lewes* (Oxford, 1890), pp. xviii *et seq.*
94. *Mon. Fran.,* I, 262.
95. *Ibid.,* I, 293.
96. *Ibid.,* I, 110, 163.
97. *Ibid.,* I, 262-3.
98. *Ibid.,* I, 264: "Quid proderit paci civium prospicere at pacem domesticorum non custodire? Attendamus quia melior est patiens viro forti, et qui dominatur animo expugnatore urbium. Miror ni prudentiae vestrae subtilitas advertat quid per hunc intendo sermonem."
99. *Ibid.,* I, 294-96.

ligation to exercise a gentle restraint over the earl,[100] expressing his regret on hearing evil reports about her conduct and insisting that she behave as became her state and dignity.[101] Such a spiritual guide was invaluable to characters like Simon and Eleanor. His place could hardly be filled.

If Simon's later advisers were of the type of the friar who wrote the *Song of Lewes,* the *Office of Simon de Montfort,* and supplied the strongly partisan information about the earl and the Barons' War contained in the *Melrose Chronicle,*[102] one does not wonder that peaceful counsel eventually gave place to more drastic action; not that the author of the *Song of Lewes* did not love peace, but he had evidently lost confidence in negotiation and the sincerity of the royal party, and felt that Simon's public spirit and integrity offered the only hope of true peace in England.[103] Simon had sought peace on the basis of liberty and reform,[104] but the only terms offered him were hanging and drawing.[105] Throughout, both the *Song of Lewes* and the *Melrose Chronicle* echo these principles: the right of constitutional liberty and liberty of the Church, and the need of curbing an arbitrary government to make it serve the best interests of the English people. Dr. Pauli's conclusion that it was the Franciscan friars who formulated the principles over which the War was fought is borne out by Mr. Kingsford: "There can be little doubt that he [the author of the *Song*] was a Franciscan friar, probably one who had been educated at Oxford under the influence of Adam Marsh and Bishop Grosseteste, and who, like the rest of his order, would have thus sympathized warmly with Earl Simon and the constitutional cause."[106]

---

100. *Ibid.,* I, 297-8.
101. *Ibid.,* I, 299.
102. Kingsford, *Song of Lewes,* pp. xx-xxiii; *Melrose Chronicle* (Edinburgh, 1835), pp. 191-216.
103. *Song of Lewes,* lines 267-8.
104. *Ibid.,* lines 226 *et seq.*
105. *Ibid.,* lines 249 *et seq.*
106. *Ibid.,* p. xviii; Pauli, *Bilder aus Alt-England,* pp. 58-9.

The principles insisted upon and the ability shown in their presentation are worthy of a university-trained friar, though the passion and rather vehement partisanship displayed are not worthy of the best type of Franciscan — an Adam Marsh, for instance. Oxford scholars of the time were not friendly to the royal cause, and probably pretty generally accepted Bracton's principle that the king is subject to the law, "for the law makes the king. Let the king then attribute to the law what the law attributes to him, namely, dominion and power. For there is no king where the will and not law has dominion."[107] This is the theme of the *Song of Lewes;* and with it Bishop Grosseteste, Adam Marsh and his *confrères* would have agreed. It is the principle insisted upon by Archbishop Pecham in his dealings with Edward I,[108] and by Friar John of Wales in his instructions to preachers of the Gospel.[109]

The author of the *Song* goes on to point out that Simon was not prompted by selfish motives; he was fighting for Church and country.[110] He subdued and captured two kings (i. e., Henry III and Richard, King of the Romans, at Lewes) because they were transgressors of the law.[111] Edward, the king's son, was unfit to rule because he was treacherous and false and put himself above the law, as if he were greater than a king: "If thou desirest the kingdom, reverence the laws."[112] "If the king be without this law, he will go astray; if he hold it not, he will err shamefully. Its presence gives right reigning, and its absence the disturbance of the realm."[113] "We give the first place to the commonalty.

---

107. Cited by C. K. Allen, *Law in the Making* (Oxford, 1927), p. 11. See also Pollock and Maitland, *The History of English Law* (Cambridge, 1895), p. 160.

108. See this essay, chap. IV.

109. *Summa collationum,* Pars Prima, Dist. III, Cap. I, *et seq.* John even goes so far as to quote with seeming approval the opinion that it is no sin, but right and just, to kill a tyrant; *loc. cit.,* chap. XX.

110. *Song of Lewes,* lines 373-75, 343 *et seq.*

111. *Ibid.,* lines 387-8.

112. *Ibid.,* lines 439 *et seq.*

113. *Ibid.,* lines 861-64; 865-70, etc.

We say also that law rules the dignity of the king; for we believe that the law is a light without which we infer that the guide goes astray."[114] The barons seek nothing contrary to the king's honor; nay, they would reform and magnify the kingly state and protect it from its enemies, the deceitful and flattering counselors who are selfishly seeking their own, till "they gradually confound the community, crush and impoverish the commonalty of the people, and subvert and infatuate the kingdom, so that no one might be able to obtain justice unless he were willing to foster the pride of such men by means of money amply bestowed."[115] "Who would endure so great a wrong?"[116]

In this manner the friar justified the rebellion of Simon, now that it had taken place, and in doing so he voiced the popular opinion and probably that of the majority of his *confrères,* many of whom looked upon their fallen hero as a saint and martyr. "After the illustrious death of this Simon," writes the Melrose chronicler, "the Friars Minorites, whom he had always loved as became a religious man, and who also were acquainted with the inmost thoughts of his heart in many respects, adopting his life as the outline of their narrative, published a history out of his excellent actions, consisting of lessons, responses, verses, hymns and other matter appertaining to the honor and respect due to a martyr; but as long as Edward survives, this compilation does not attain that acceptance, by being chanted within the Church of God, which was anticipated."[117]

---

114. *Ibid.,* lines 847-50.

115. *Ibid.,* lines 527 *et seq.,* 566-71 *et seq.*

116. *Ibid.,* line 572.

117. *Chronica de Mailros* (Edinburgh, 1825), p. 212; translation of the Rev. Jos. Stevenson in *The Church Historians of England,* IV (London, 1856), p. 233.

Regarding this office see Kingsford, *Song of Lewes,* pp. xxi-xxiii; and G. W. Prothero, *Simon de Montfort* (London, 1877), pp. 388-91, where part of the office is printed. The oration reads: "Deus, qui beatum symonem martyrem tuum virtutem constancie in agone suo communisti, quique illi ad renovandum britanniae regnum milites inclitos associasti, tribue nos eius precibus adiuvari qui celebri martyrio meruit consummari."

The royalist author of the *Flores historiarum* singles out the Franciscans for special reproach as ingrates toward the king and the Pope because they supported the rebels "by the flatteries of their preaching and approbation."[118]

But such testimony, even after its possible bias has been discounted, is apt to give a false coloring to the actual position taken by the great body of the Friars Minor. We must have regard to the highly individualistic character of the Franciscans. There is more than an inherent improbability in the view that the Franciscans as a group were actively engaged in preaching rebellion, much as they may have agreed with the general principles for which the barons fought. Adam Marsh's letters show that only a few years before the open conflict the friars were on familiar terms with royalists as well as non-royalists. And in a fight in which the barons themselves wavered and changed sides, it is not to be expected that the friars would have offered a firm and united front. As late as 1255 the royalist William de Valence, as we have seen,[119] engaged a Franciscan confessor for himself and his family. Roger Bacon's family were staunch royalists, and Roger's own sympathies were probably with the king's party.[120] Both before and after the war members of both sides were benefactors of the Franciscans; and there seems to be no sufficient evidence that Henry III, Edward or any of the other members of the royal family harbored ill will against the Franciscans as a body at any time.[121] According to one account, Edward even took refuge with the friars after the defeat at Lewes.[122] In view of these facts, Mr. Kingsford's theory regarding the author of the *Song of Lewes,* the *Office of Simon de Montfort,* and the account

---

118. Rolls Series, III, 266.

119. See this chapter, p. 54.

120. *Opera adhuc inedita, Opus Tertium,* R. S., p. 16; also Prof. Brewer's remarks, p. xiv.

121. See this chapter, pp. 50 *et seq.,* and chap. IV.

122. *The Metrical Chronicle of Robert of Gloucester,* R. S., p. 750, lines 11, 388-89. Even if this is not true, there remains the fact that Robert found nothing out of place in his doing so.

of Simon in the *Melrose Chronicle,* appears the more plausible, namely, that one friar was responsible and that banishment was the price he paid for his violent partisanship.[123]

We must likewise beware of broad generalizations to the effect that, whereas the Franciscans supported the baronial faction, the Dominicans supported the king. It is true that the Dominican John Darlington was at this time Henry III's confessor,[124] defended the royal cause in the Oxford parliament held in the Black Friars' convent in 1258, served as a royalist appointee on the reform committee of twenty-four,[125] received Simon's peace delegates to the king before the battle of Lewes,[126] and was instrumental in obtaining royal favors for his *confrères* at a time when the Friars Minor seem to have been somewhat neglected.[127] Nevertheless, it must be remembered that Simon de Montfort had friends among the Dominicans as well as among the Franciscans and other religious. Dominicans, Franciscans and seculars are numbered among those who gave testimony to the miracles supposed to have been wrought by the popular martyr of Evesham.[128] Dominicans, Franciscans, Carmelites and Trinitarians shared in the bequests of Amaury de Montfort.[129] Simon's wife Eleanor spent her declining years with the Augustinian nuns of St. Dominic at Montargis, France.[130] Though Pope Clement IV's legate Ottoboni, in 1266, seemed to imply that the Franciscans were special offenders against the peace of the realm,[131] both he and his predecessor were empowered to compel, if necessary by ecclesiastical censures, the Friars Preachers and Minor and other religious to assist them in their mission of pacification.[132] In spite of

---

123. *Song of Lewes,* pp. xx-xxiii.
124. *The Antiquary,* London, XXII, 115.
125. *Grey Friars in Oxford,* p. 72.
126. Treharne, *The Baronial Plan of Reform,* pp. 306-7.
127. *Cal. Pat., 1258-1266,* pp. 508, 514.
128. *Miracles of Simon de Montfort,* Camden Soc., XV, 77-110.
129. *Grey Friars in Oxford,* pp. 102-3.
130. Bémont-Jacob, *Simon de Montfort* (Oxford, 1930), pp. 258-9.
131. *Eng. Hist. Review,* XV, 99.
132. *Cal. Papal Letters,* I, 396-98; 410-11, 427-8.

the papal excommunication against Simon and his followers, prelates, clergy and religious were divided in their loyalties.

There appears to be more reason, as we shall see, to draw a line between the political affiliations of Franciscans and Dominicans during Edward II's troubles with his barons, but by this time both orders had lost much of their old spiritual fervor, and Queen Isabella's close friendship with the Franciscans would in part account for their support of her against the weak and unfortunate king.[133]

As a final illustration of the influence exerted by the Franciscans upon the governing class in England, we give the case of Friar Henry of Wodestone and the legislation against the Jews. Though the friars had once been instrumental in saving condemned Jews from death,[134] they could not approve of some of the practices of which the Jews were guilty and in which they were protected by the king and his ministers. Before the law, the Jew in medieval England was the ward of the king, who used him to replenish his all-too-frequently depleted treasury. The Jew had a monopoly on lending money at interest; and people paid him as high as 43 percent on the money they borrowed. Gradually, Jews became holders of land on a large scale, and claimed the privileges attached thereto — even the wardship and marriages of infant heirs among their tenants, and the right to present clerks to Christian churches.[135] In 1271 these claims led to a crisis.

Sir Geoffrey of Childwick, a knight who held the Manor of Childwick in Hertfordshire of St. Alban's Abbey, became a debtor to a Jew named Cok, son of Cresseus. On Geoffrey's death, his heir enfeoffed Cok with the abbey lands before the abbot could assume the debt of four hundred pounds owing to the Jew.

---

133. See chap. IV, *passim.*

134. See chap. II, p. 42, 43.

135. Pollock and Maitland, *The History of English Law,* pp. 451-56; Walsingham, *Gesta abbatum,* R. S., I, 401; *Liber de antiquis legibus,* Camden Soc., vol. 34, p. 234.

It had been previously arranged that the abbot was to retain the lands, but the Jews contested the case; and it looked as if they would win it, together with the right of wardship over Christian minors on their lands and the presentation to church livings. Their hand was strengthened by the fact that Queen Eleanor had a claim on the manor and appeared to favor the Jews, while other influential persons, moved by bribes or fear, also took their side. Suddenly a Friar Minor, Henry of Wodestone, appeared before the king and his council and showed by convincing arguments that it was wrong and disgraceful to subject Christians and ecclesiastical livings to Jews in this manner. As a consequence a statute was passed denying Jews the privileges they sought with such determination.[136]

However, pressure on the part of the Jews was apparently delaying the publication of the law, till the two brothers, Walter Giffard (Archbishop of York) and Godfrey Giffard (Bishop of Worcester), wrote a strongly worded letter to Richard Stanes the justiciar, urging that he secure the cöoperation of the chancellor, justices of the bench and others favorable to the law, so that it might be enrolled and published. The Giffards warned the justiciar that they would tolerate no trifling, in spite of those who might try to modify the statute. As Dr. Little points out, both archbishop and bishop were friends of the Franciscans, and it seems fairly evident that their vigorous action was prompted by Friar Henry. The arguments used in their letter are, often word for word, the same as those prepared by the friar.[137] The protest was effective and the statute was issued July 25, 1271.[138]

---

136. *Gesta abbatum,* I, 400 *et seq.; Liber de antiquis legibus,* p. 234; Dr. Little discusses the whole case in *Collectanea Franciscana* (B. S. F. S., X), pp. 150 *et seq.*

137. Dr. Little, *op. cit.,* pp. 153-4, and other works cited above. Compare MS. Bodley 91, fol. 140: *Contra Judeos per quendam fratrum minorum.* The manuscript records the decision of the council as well as Friar Henry's arguments before it. It is probably a rough draft for the statute or for the letter.

138. *Cal. Pat., 1266-1272,* p. 598; Rymer, *Foedera,* p. 489.

IV

THE FRIARS AND THE KING

Hundreds of entries in the Patent Rolls, Close Rolls, Chancery Warrants and Wardrobe Accounts during practically the entire century and a quarter with which we are here concerned testify to the cordial relations which existed between the Franciscans and the royal family. The numerous grants of food, clothing, fuel, money, sites and materials for building, exemptions from taxes, protection and the like tell on the one hand of the royal bounty and good-will; requests for prayers, for preachers of crusades, summonses to parliament and commissions to important embassies tell on the other hand how the friars on their part repaid their royal benefactors by faithful service. These grants to the friars are our only evidence of the existence of certain friaries, and our only means of dating the foundation of others, or of determining the number of friars occupying them.[1] They frequently assume a routine character, like the grants to hospitals and other charitable foundations. Or they might be included in dispensations of charity to the poor, but the great number of them indicates how completely the Franciscans had impressed their utility upon the minds of reigning sovereigns.

As with the burghers and barons, this royal munificence was the world's way of expressing its appreciation of heroic ideals and unselfish devotion to humanity. But while it contributed generously to the material needs of the friars, the world was, ironically, in its bungling way helping to undermine the very ideals it so much admired. We have an early example of this in the chapel which Henry III built for the Franciscans at Reading. Because

1. See Eccleston, edited by Little, pp. 149 *et seq.; Studies in English Franciscan History,* pp. 68 et seq.

the building violated his conception of Franciscan poverty, the minister general, Albert of Pisa, on his visitation about 1236, not daring to tear it down "on account of the lord king who had built it, wished that heaven might destroy it."[2] On account of the objections of the townsmen, Albert had only with difficulty succeeded in destroying the stone enclosure of the Southampton convent;[3] with the king as benefactor, resistance was particularly difficult. Though the friars showed on occasion that they could stand firm on principle even at the risk of royal displeasure,[4] favor from high places naturally placed them under obligation. The danger was a subtle one, and it was not easy to draw the line where the recognition of favors must stop.

The York friary might be cited as an illustration. When the English province was divided into custodies about the middle of the thirteenth century, York was made the center of one of them. The first custos, Friar Martin de Barton, insisted that none of the friaries under him should have more inmates than could be supported on alms alone, such was his devotion to holy poverty.[5] King Henry was a benefactor of the first friary in York,[6] as well as of the larger foundation begun in 1243.[7] Edward I continued the royal benefactions toward the York friars,[8] as did Edward II and Queen Isabella.[9] For a time during 1319-1320 the king dwelt in the friary and received his officials there.[10] Some of the sessions of the York parliament of 1322 were evidently held in the Franciscan church,[11] and during this time it was that

---

2. Eccleston, p. 100.
3. *Ibid.*, p. 99.
4. See chap. II, 46; chap. III, pp. 58-60, 68,69; this chap., *passim.*
5. Eccleston, p. 44.
6. *Close Rolls, 1234-1237,* pp. 224, 497, 498.
7. Eccleston, p. 56; *Cal. Liberate Rolls, 1240-1245,* p. 217; *Cal. Pat., 1266-1272,* pp. 260-61.
8. *Cal. Pat. 1301-1307,* p. 387.
9. *Victoria County Histories,* Yorks., III, 288-9; *Cal. Pat., 1313-1317,* p. 166.
10. *Cal. Close, 1318-1323,* pp. 219-20; *1323-1327,* p. 127.
11. *Cal. Pat., 1321-1324,* p. 142.

the king sent the guardian and a companion to visit the captive John of Brittany in Scotland.[12]

Edward III was particularly fond of staying with the friars. On his way to the Scottish war in 1327 he spent about six weeks in the York convent; and the queen mother, Isabella, maintained a separate suite there at the same time, on one occasion entertaining as many as sixty ladies at a feast in the friars' dormitory.[13] Edward reimbursed the brethren for the material "damages" done,[14] but it is doubtful if the spiritual harm suffered from these invasions was so easily repaired. In 1335 the king gave orders that one hundred shillings be spent in repairs on his York castle, house and pond, "and a certain wall and spring in the garden of the Minorites near the door of the kitchen to be repaired and amended for the king's easement when he shall stay there."[15] And stay there he did that same year, for "in the chamber of the Friars Minor of York where the king was lodging" the chancellor surrendered to him the Great Seal in the presence of the treasurer and many other prominent officials.[16]

If the York friary was the center of so much attention on the part of the royal family, it is not surprising that in London, the capital of the kingdom, the Franciscans should have been particularly singled out. It is not necessary to enumerate the many regular grants of food, clothing and the rest of which they were the recipients from the king's treasury, or to recall how the royal family took the Poor Clares under their special patronage.[17] To understand somewhat how the Franciscans stood in relation to the country's rulers, it is sufficient to consider the magnificent Grey Friars' Church which rose up in London during the four-

---

12. See chap. III, p. 55.
13. S. Luce, ed., *Froissart's Chronicle* (Paris, 1869), I, 44-5.
14. *Victoria County Histories*, Yorks., III, 289.
15. *Cal. Close, 1333-1337,* p. 379; *Cal. Pat., 1334-1348,* p. 85.
16. *Cal. Close, 1333-1337,* p. 493.
17. See chap. II, pp. 38, 39, and references; also *Cal. Pat., 1313-1317,* p. 449; *1338-1340,* p. 467; *1345-1348,* pp. 125, 410; *Cal. Close, 1330-1333,* p. 466; *1343-1346,* p. 177.

teenth century. The Patent Rolls of May, 1269, suggest the great building operations in which the friars were engaged already at that time.[18] When the new church was abuilding three-quarters of a century later, the king granted protection for "the guardian and Friars Minor of London and men and servants whom they are sending with ships, boats, carts and other carriages to divers parts for stone, timber and other things necessary for the fabric of their church and repair of their house."[19]

The so-called "new church," we know, was begun in 1306, when William Walden laid the foundation stone in the name of Queen Margaret, second wife of Edward I. Margaret contributed two thousand marks toward its construction during her lifetime and left one hundred marks in her will for the same purpose. Though built and furnished by the joint contributions of royal personages, nobility and townsmen, the church was primarily a monument to the members of ruling families. Queen Isabella, wife of the unfortunate Edward II, was the most generous benefactor, giving over seven hundred pounds to the building. Edward III paid for the renovation of the large central window, and his wife, Queen Philippa, was likewise a generous contributor to the structure.[20]

The finished edifice, three hundred feet in length, ninety-five feet in width and sixty-four feet in height, with marble columns and floors and glazed windows, was a worthy resting-place for its noble patrons, though hardly representative of the ideals of St. Francis. There is an apologetic note in the opening words of the friar chronicler's account of the new church: "To the perpetual memory of the founders and helpers of this church, to relieve the wonder of certain persons who are amazed at the struc-

---

18. *Cal. Pat., 1266-1272,* p. 339.

19. *Cal. Pat., 1343-1345,* p. 476. Also see *1345-1348,* p. 27.

20. "Prima fundatio," *Mon. Fran.,* I, 513 *et seq.;* E. B. S. Shepherd, "The Church of the Friars Minor in London," *The Archaeological Journal,* LIX, 238, *et seq.;* C. L. Kingsford, *The Grey Friars of London,* pp. 30 *et seq.,* 150 *et seq.*

ture and do not know whence its costs have been drawn."[21] Among the seven hundred and sixty-five prominent persons who were buried in the church in the course of several centuries, there were Queens Margaret and Isabella of England, Mary (Isabella?), Queen of Man, and Joan, Queen of Scotland (wife of David Bruce); the heart of Queen Eleanor (wife of Henry III) and the heart of Edward II were also interred there.[22] Regarding the former, the *Lanercost Chronicle* gives an interesting account. Queen Eleanor's burial had been postponed a long time in order that King Edward I might be able to attend, and "when her body was committed to the earth with much pomp, King Edward, with his own hand, gave his mother's heart, encased in gold, to her relative, the Minister General of the Friars Minor, staying in the English province at the time, with these words: 'I commit to thee as the nearest relation of my mother the dearest treasure I have; and do thou bury it honorably amongst thy brethren in London, whom she loved more than any others in this world."[23] The London Grey Friars' Church was one of the places where services were conducted for the repose of the soul of Edward I's consort, Eleanor, as she was being carried to burial;[24] her heart, however, was laid to rest with the Dominicans.[25]

We said that the Franciscans repaid the royal favor by faithful service. As far as spiritual guidance is concerned, they were evidently more sought by the queens than by the kings, which partially explains the fact that the queens were more generous toward their London church. Whereas practically all the kings from Henry III to Henry VI had Dominican confessors,[26] the

21. "Prima fundatio," *Mon. Fran.*, I, 513.
22. Shepherd in *Archaeological Journal,* LIX, 266 *et seq.;* Kingsford, *Grey Friars of London,* pp. 70 *et seq.*
23. *Lanercost Chronicle,* p. 141.
24. Kingsford, *op. cit.,* p. 17; "Annales Londonienses," *Chronicles of the Reigns of Edward I and Edward II,* R. S., I, 99.
25. *Lanercost Chronicle,* p. 138; "Annales Londonienses," *loc. cit.*
26. *The Antiquary,* XXII, 114-20, 159-60, 262-66; XXIII, 24-6. Edward IV evidently had a Franciscan confessor, at least for a time; see Kingsford, *Grey Friars of London,* p. 79.

queens, at least for the period here treated, seem to have been more generally inclined to the Franciscans for guidance. Queen Eleanor, wife of Henry III, was a close friend and correspondent of Adam Marsh,[27] and requested the Franciscan William Batale to attend her.[28] We know that Henry III made special provision for the Franciscans who dwelt at his court.[29] Queen Isabella, wife of Edward II, had the Franciscans Robert Lamborn and John Vye as confessors.[30] The Franciscan John Mablethorpe (Malberthorp) was confessor to Queen Philippa;[31] and Queen Margaret of Scotland, sister of Edward I, also had a Franciscan confessor.[32]

It is remarkable how completely the two chief mendicant orders, the Dominicans and Franciscans, captivated the hearts of kings and queens, as well as of the nobility and populace. The jealous eye of Matthew Paris was quick to note, not only that the people were won by the friars,[33] but that they had become the "counselors and messengers of the great ones,"[34] "counselors of kings and special emissaries, so that, whereas formerly those dressed in soft garments were in the houses of kings, now those who are dressed in mean clothes are in the houses, the chambers and the palaces of princes."[35] The friars have become "counselors, valets-de-chambre and treasurers in the courts of kings and potentates."[36] As early as 1233, when the friars intervened in the troubles between Henry III and his earl marshal, Matthew Paris noted that the king "was accustomed to venerate and heed" them.[37]

---

27. *Mon. Fran.*, I, 288-91, 307-14.
28. *Ibid.*, 332.
29. *Liberate Roll of Henry III, 1250,* reprinted in Eccleston, edited by Little, p. 177.
30. Kingsford, *Grey Friars of London,* pp. 75, 79.
31. *Ibid.*, p. 56; *Cal. Pat., 1367-1370,* p. 432.
32. *Lanercost Chronicle,* p. 97. The chronicler praises her virtue and the edifying way she prepared for death in 1274-1275; Adam Marsh commemorated her marriage in 1251 (*Mon. Fran.*, I, 107).
33. *Chron. maj.*, III, 332-34; IV, 279.
34. *Ibid.*, III, 333.
35. *Ibid.*, III, 627.
36. *Ibid.*, IV, 279.
37. *Ibid.*, III, 251.

Blessed Agnellus of Pisa, founder of the English province, was one of the friars whom the king venerated and heeded at this time.[38] And there were others of his order. Unfortunately, not all of them were of the same mettle as Agnellus, and again we get examples of the dangers which lay in the work of the Franciscans, especially in too great royal favor. Agnellus was obliged to remove a friar "secretary to the king" from court and to forbid him to give or receive presents.[39] Another friar, Ralph de Rose, "became very intimate with the Lord King of England through the exceeding great charm of his preaching, but his end proved how displeasing to God is the friendship of this world and how contrary it is to the simplicity of the Order of Friars Minor to be lifted up by the favor of the great and to dwell constantly in the courts of princes."[40]

Neither the danger nor the complaint was new. Thomas of Celano denounced the ambition, idleness and luxurious living of court-dwelling friars in Italy.[41] No matter what the opportunities for good offered by their position, there were naturally strong temptations to relax the rule of poverty and mortification in surroundings of ease and luxury. Sometimes there were good reasons to make concessions to the friars who accompanied rulers, and dispensations from certain observances were legally obtained. For example, the Pope dispensed friars who were to accompany Henry III "beyond the sea" from the rule which forbade them

---

38. Roger Wendover, *Chronicle,* R. S., III, 64.

39. Eccleston, p. 97.

40. *Ibid.,* p. 38. Though his Franciscan spirit suffered from his court life, Friar Ralph seems not to have ended so badly as Eccleston would have us suppose. He became a papal penitentiary under Gregory IX and ended a long life in the Roman Curia (*Mon. Fran.,* I, 549).

41. Edouard d'Alencon, ed., *S. Francisci Assisiensis vita et miracula* (Rome, 1906), II, 261-62.

St. Thomas Aquinas defends the dwelling at court of friars by adducing such examples as Joseph and Daniel from the Old Testament. He condemns, however, those who dwell there for motives of honor or pleasure instead of God's glory, the motive of saints. See *Opusculum XIX* (Parma edn., *Opusc. I*) in Fr. John Proctor, *An Apology for the Religious Orders* (London, 1902), pp. 329-33.

to ride horseback.[42] Adam Marsh asked for a similar dispensation for Gregory de Bosellis while he accompanied the Archbishop of Canterbury.[43] But these and like concessions[44] were not the real dangers, which were much more subtle. Only men of solid character and deep spirituality would be likely to endure for long the life in a worldly court without suffering harm; and it must have been very hard for such friars afterward to settle down to the routine and simplicity of life in a friary. Thus we have Queen Isabella obtaining papal permission for her old confessor, Robert Lamborn, to "remain in the place of the Friars Minor in London, where he now is, and have a decent room therein for life, and a companion of the said order, with a clerk and two servants at his disposal, and have his books about him, and other things which he had from the said queen, in whose service he was for sixteen years, he being now infirm and nearly blind. If necessary he may transfer himself to any other English house of the order."[45] All the Dominican confessors of the kings received an annual grant on their retirement,[46] as did the Franciscan confessor of Queen Philippa.[47] It was probably the abuse of such privileges as these which caused Eccleston to moralize about the end of Friar Ralph, who may have lost the spirit of a friar without ceasing to be useful in the service of the Church.

Such were the hazards of the Franciscan life, the flame and smoke to which the friars were exposed in their attempt to extinguish a conflagration.[48] A few failures or partial failures must not blind us to the excellent work they were doing as a body; for there were many who, like Friar Agnellus, could move in court circles and remain strict Franciscans. Adam Marsh was certainly

42. *Bullarium Franciscanum,* I, 542.
43. *Mon. Fran.,* I, 368-69.
44. *Cal. Papal Letters,* I, 305; II, 243, recording papal dispensations from the rule of silence at table for Dominicans at the English court.
45. *Cal. Papal Letters,* III, 88.
46. *The Antiquary,* vols. XXII, XXIII, *locis citatis.*
47. *Cal. Pat., 1367-1370,* p. 432.
48. See chap. II, p. 40.

such a one. His friends, William Batale, William Bellun[49] and Gregory de Bosellis[50] were evidently of the same type. The Lanercost chronicler assures us that King Henry called Adam "Father" and did many things on his advice,[51] though Adam must have told him at times things that were not pleasant to hear. "About the feast of St. Luke [October 18, probably in 1250]," Adam wrote to Simon de Montfort, "I incurred a rising of the royal indignation, as I think, on account of words of life. For which reason I am not permitted to enter the presence of the lord king or the queen. The Lord's will be done."[52] How long this banishment lasted we do not know. Likely it was only for a brief period, for both the king and queen thought too highly of Adam's character and ability. Certain it is that Adam was again on good terms with the king in 1257, when Henry sent him on an embassy to France,[53] and sought to have him appointed to the bishopric of Ely.[54]

Adam was active in affairs of the state as early as 1247, when he was sent with the prior provincial of the Dominicans on a mission of the king.[55] This same year he succeeded Thomas Wallensis as lector of the Franciscans at Oxford;[56] and from that time till his death in 1258 he stands out as one of the great Englishmen of his age. His influence in the councils of Church and State, as well as in the affairs of the University of Oxford and those of his province and order, can be partially estimated from his varied correspondence. But what would we not give for a collection of the letters of his correspondents! Or would that he had dared to write more plainly about matters which so vitally affected the history of his day! What was the subject of his con-

49. *Mon. Fran.*, I, 292, 332, 401.
50. See chap. III, p. 62.
51. *Lanercost Chronicle,* p. 24.
52. *Mon. Fran.*, I, 275.
53. *Cal. Pat., 1247-1258,* p. 594, cf. p. 609; *Close Rolls, 1256-1259,* p. 197.
54. Matthew Paris, *Chron. maj.*, V, 619, 635.
55. Little, *Grey Friars in Oxford,* p. 137.
56. *Ibid.*, p. 136.

versations with the king at Oxford, the issue of which was so grave as to call for the "highest courage"?[57] What was his trying business with the queen "affecting the king and his heirs"?[58] What was the urgent business "touching the scepter of the realm" on which he was summoned to London?[59]

Adam's influence with the queen was undoubtedly great, and was probably responsible for her decision to cöoperate with Bishop Grosseteste's reform efforts by presenting only worthy clerks.[60] The queen appealed to Adam to use his influence with the minister provincial so that Friar William Batale might be sent to attend her,[61] and wrote to him affectionately and urgently to visit her at the first opportunity, though Adam found the request difficult and troublesome.[62] The importunities of the king and queen and the Archbishop of Canterbury prevented Adam from accompanying Bishop Grosseteste to Rome in 1250.[63] The queen seconded the request of the archbishop that Adam accompany him, but at that time the king looked upon Adam as a traitorous enemy (most likely on account of his support of Simon de Montfort and Bishop Grosseteste) and forbade the archbishop to have Adam about him.[64] Far from being disappointed, the friar found the king's opposition a godsend,[65] and went so far as to obtain a papal privilege by which he could not be forced to give his services to any prelate or prince.[66] No wonder, for he was advancing in age, and the demands made upon him from all quarters taxed him beyond endurance. Besides his university work and his constant correspondence, he was on a commission to arbitrate difficulties between the king and the Bishop of St. David's

57. *Mon. Fran.*, I, 141-2.
58. *Ibid.*, I, p. 152.
59. *Ibid.*, p. 387.
60. *Ibid.*, p. 116; cf. pp. 293-4.
61. *Ibid.*, p. 332.
62. *Ibid.*, p. 311.
63. *Ibid.*, p. 312.
64. *Ibid.*, pp. 334-9, 342.
65. *Ibid.*, p. 342.
66. *Ibid.*, p. 335.

and other difficulties between this same bishop and the Abbot of Gloucester; and Simon de Montfort and his countess were demanding his presence on urgent matters. The strain of it all was beginning to be felt.[67]

As pointed out in the preceding chapter, the period following the death of Adam Marsh was one in which relations between the king and some of the Franciscans became strained. Adam's own difficulties with Henry were but a prelude to a more violent clash when peaceful counsel ceased to prevail.[68] But whatever the relations between king and friar during the Barons' War, no bad blood prevailed between them after order was restored. Beginning with 1266, the king's liberality to the Franciscans appears to go on as before.[69] Not only Henry, but Richard of Cornwall and Lord Edward continued to show their affection for the friars. In 1269 Richard granted the Chichester Franciscans his so-called Old Castle as a dwelling,[70] and the following year the Franciscan William of Heddele and perhaps others, accompanied Edward on his crusade to Syria.[71] An entry in the Patent Rolls of 1271 further indicates Edward's and the king's regard for the Friars Minor. "Whereas Edward the king's son," it reads, "lately observed the narrowness of the place where the Friars Minor in the town of Yarmouth are lodged, he besought the king to ask the bailiffs and good men of that town to grant them a lane on the north side, and they at the king's instance have granted it to them; the king accepts this grant and grants that the friars may hold it and build upon it, and has taken them and their buildings into his special protection."[72] And we shall see that Edward remained friendly to the Franciscans throughout his reign. For the

---

67. *Ibid.*, pp. 334-39, 342-3.
68. See chap. III, pp. 59 *et seq.*
69. See, e. g., *Cal. Pat., 1258-1266.* p. 603; *1266-1272,* pp. 113, 320, 339, etc.
70. *Cal. Pat., 1266-1272,* p. 369.
71. *Lanercost Chronicle,* p. 81. Though given under 1266, Edward's departure was really in 1270. See also Golubovich, *Biblioteca bio-bibliografica,* I, 280, 281; II, 413.
72. *Cal Pat., 1266-1272,* p. 530.

present we must turn back to the period immediately preceding the baronial disturbances.

This period, between 1247 and 1263, is marked by the number of Franciscans who came to England as papal delegates or nuncios. The first who are mentioned are John and Alexander. They came in 1247 to collect funds for the papal treasury. Matthew Paris recounts the trouble they had with the monks of St. Albans, who finally acceded to the demands for money when John returned the same year with increased papal powers to compel obedience.[73] In 1248 John, whom Paris describes as an Englishman, was collector of the Holy Land subsidy in England, Ireland and Scotland, and a *confrère,* William, was his sub-collector in Scotland.[74] Two years later John was again active in England as a papal nuncio;[75] and it must have been at this time that Adam Marsh corresponded with him and urged him to call on Bishop Grosseteste on important business, in which Adam expected to join.[76] In 1256 John (de Cantia) appears as one of the executors of the business of the Cross in England;[77] and in 1258 he was engaged as a papal nuncio in negotiating a loan for

73. *Chron. maj.,* V, 599, 600, 617.

74. *Bullarium Fran.,* I, 509-10; *Cal. Papal Letters,* I, 243. William, whose last name is variously written Basynges, Batinches or Bafinches, was probably also an Englishman resident for a time in London (Kingsford, *Grey Friars of London,* p. 158).

Much confusion exists as to the identity of Friar John: see Wadding, *Annales,* III, 213, 403-5 and his *Scriptores Ordinis Minorum* (Rome, 1806), p. 129, and Sbaralea's supplement, p. 386. The problem is whether John Anglicus, John de Cantia, and John de Dya (or Dyva) are one, two or three persons. Since Paris expressly says that the John who came to England in 1247 was an Englishman, *de Cantia oriundus* (*Chron. maj.,* V, 599; *Hist. Anglorum,* III, 18, 298), and Grosseteste spoke to John de Dya as to one from a foreign land (Eccleston, p. 114); furthermore, since entries in the Patent Rolls almost side by side appear to distinguish between John de Cantia and John de Dyva, I think we may safely count them as two. Cf. *Cal. Pat., 1247-1258,* pp. 470 and 471, and Father Cuthbert's argument to the contrary, *The Chronicle of Thomas Eccleston* (London, 1909), pp. 129, 130. As I see no sufficient reason to distinguish between John de Cantia and John Anglicus, I have applied Ockham's razor in my treatment of them.

75. *Cal. Papal Letters,* I, 263.

76. *Mon. Fran.,* I, 386. See also Letters 173, 217, 218, etc.

77. *Cal. Pat., 1247-1258,* p. 470, also p. 498.

King Henry wherewith to pay a two-years' cess to the Pope.[78] From that time till 1266 it appears to have been his unpleasant task to collect this yearly cess from the king in order to pay back the merchants who had advanced the money to the Pope. At least he was so engaged in 1261 and 1262.[79] In July, 1263, he was again appointed papal nuncio to succeed Master Leonard,[80] and in this capacity he was ordered by the Pope to put Henry's chapel under interdict if the king did not pay up his annual cess of one thousand marks then due for three years.[81] In November of the same year John was still representing the Pope in England.[82] We hear nothing of him between the battles of Lewes and Evesham; but in 1266 he was again at his task of compelling the king to pay his marks.[83]

John de Dyva's career was largely contemporary with that of John de Cantia.[84] He was one of Henry III's envoys to the Roman court in 1241,[85] negotiated between Henry and Pope Alexander IV in the Sicilian affair in 1255,[86] played a part in the negotiations following Richard of Cornwall's election as King of the Romans,[87] and was still active as a papal penitentiary in

78. *Ibid.*, p. 631.
79. *Cal. Papal Letters,* I, 380, 384.
80. *Ibid.*, p. 386.
81. *Ibid.*, pp. 379, 387.
82. *Ibid.*, p. 393.
83. *Ibid.*, p. 424.
84. The first clear reference to John Anglicus or de Cantia is 1247, the last, 1266; the first to John de Dyva is 1241, the last 1256. See note 74, p. 81.
85. *Cal. Pat., 1232-1247,* p. 245. The fact that John was chosen to represent Henry on this occasion would argue for his being an Englishman. It may be that Grosseteste's reference to John's country as if it were foreign is best explained by either supposing that John was dwelling in Rome in the service of the Pope, or identifying him after all with the John who came to England in 1247 and who, according to Matthew Paris, was at that time minister provincial of Provence. See *Chron. maj.* V, 617. I confess that I am unable to clarify the problem.

John de Dyva was sent to England in 1254 by Innocent IV to investigate abuses of patronage (*Bullarium Franciscanum,* I, 689, 690), and Matthew Paris, under the year 1256, commends him for his work (*Chron. maj.*, V, 568). Paris was rather hard on John the Englishman in his *Chronica major* (V, 599, 600, 617), but quite mild in his *Historia Anglorum* (III, 18).

86. *Foedera,* I, 328.
87. *Annales monastici,* I, 392.

England in 1256, when he interceded for a certain burgess of Rochester who had helped a man to escape from prison.[88]

Following John de Dyva, other Franciscans came to England as papal envoys. Friar Mansuetus was sent by Pope Alexander IV in 1257 to negotiate peace between England and France.[89] The next year, according to Matthew Paris,[90] Mansuetus came again at Henry's request, armed with extensive powers for furthering the Sicilian venture. While in England at this time he was instrumental in procuring pardon for several men involved in charges of murder.[91] In 1259 Friar Velascus, a penitentiary of the Franciscan Order, was also sent to England by Alexander IV as nuncio. His entrance was procured by Henry in violation of the rights claimed by the Provisional Government, and the barons appealed against him to the Pope when he defended the right of Aylmer of Valence to the see of Winchester.[92] In 1260 another Franciscan, Friar Walter, came to England "on an embassage from the Pope to the King of Almain,"[93] and the following year he was there again for the purpose of preparing a synod of the English clergy.[94]

All this was in keeping with the rôles being played by friars in other parts of Europe at the same time.[95] But the friars were used as emissaries by others than the Pope. A Franciscan and a Dominican served on a delegation to Henry III from Bordeaux

---

88. *Cal. Pat., 1247-1258,* p. 471.

89. *Foedera,* I, 21. The letter of appointment is wrongly dated by Rymer, but the mistake is corrected by Hardy in his *Syllabus of Rymer's Foedera* (London, 1869), I, 60. Cf. Potthast, *Regesta,* II, 1390; and Jaffre, *Regesta,* II, 160.

90. *Chron. maj.,* V, 679-80; also 685-86.

91. *Cal. Pat., 1247-1258,* pp. 626-7.

92. *Cal. Pat., 1258-1266,* pp. 35, 43, 113, 132; "An Unauthorized Use of the Great Seal," *Eng. Hist. Review,* XL, 403-11. On Velascus see also Wadding, *Annales Minorum,* III, 335, 387-8.

93. *Cal. Pat., 1258-1266,* p. 120.

94. *Flores historiarum,* II, 465, 468-9. He is called Walter Reigate here and in Eccleston, pp. 102-3. Possibly his was but a single mission lasting from 1260 to 1261.

95. See Paris, *Chron. maj.,* IV, 612, 635; III, 628, 636, etc.; Koch, *Die fruehesten Niederlassungen der Minoriten,* etc., pp. 94-5, 99, 113, etc.

in 1257.[96] Two Franciscans, John de Bekingham and Geoffrey de Fugeriis, were sent by Edward I to Norway in 1290 to complete the negotiations for the marriage of Edward II to Margaret, the young Queen of Scotland, and to bring the queen to her future home.[97] In 1297 the Franciscan, Friar Ivoer, was one of the delegates to King Edward from the King of Norway.[98] Irish Franciscans were sent to Edward II in 1325 "to show some things touching the state of that land," and the king instructed his officials to "attend well to what they have to say."[99] The following year two Spanish Friars Minor, Peter Oliverii and Berengar Foulcrandy, bore letters and a secret message to Edward from Peter, "the youngest infant of the King of Aragon," and Edward "heard them joyfully and with good-will" and sent them back with his message.[100]

Thus in the records of the Middle Ages we constantly meet the barefoot, grey-clad Friar Minor traveling to and fro between courts and rulers. Universally trusted and respected, and eschewing wealth and power, the friars in their early days made ideal envoys. It was not unnatural either that their services should be desired for high positions in the Church at a time when ecclesiastics played such an important part in civil as well as church government. But both Francis and Dominic had rejected the suggestion that their spiritual sons assume ecclesiastical dignities,[101] and the English friars on the whole were successful in avoiding bishoprics. The two Franciscans who held sees in England during the thirteenth century received their appointments following a period of theological lecturing to the cardinals of

---

96. *Cal. Pat., 1247-1258,* p. 608.

97. Rev. Jos. Stevenson, *Documents Illustrative of the History of Scotland* (Edinburgh, 1870), I, 138-9, 142, 145.

98. *Cal. Pat., 1292-1301,* p. 255. The *Lanercost Chronicle,* p. 104, tells how attached was the Norwegian royal family to the Franciscans, and how the king took an interest in their schools.

99. *Cal. Chancery Warrants, 1244-1326,* p. 561.

100. *Cal. Close, 1323-1327,* p. 547; *Cal. Pat., 1324-1327,* p. 245.

101. Celano, *S. Francisci Assisiensis vita et miracula,* edited by Edouard d'Alencon, pp. 280-282.

the Roman Curia.[102] And both of them proved to be not only great churchmen, but great influences in the affairs of state and society as well.

Friar John Pecham, who became Archbishop of Canterbury in 1279, had acted as one of the king's delegates in the settlement of a dispute at the University of Oxford in 1275,[103] though his first meeting with Edward is said to have been at the peace conference at Amiens in 1279. If Edward was pleased with Pecham's correct English attitude on this occasion,[104] he was soon to learn that the new archbishop had no intention of being the subservient tool of high-handed royal action at home. Immediately on his arrival in England, Pecham summoned a council of his clergy at Reading and began the reforms he had been sent to carry out.[105] Among other things, he insisted upon the observance of the Magna Carta and the freedom of the Church from royal encroachments.[106] And though the king successfully demanded the deletion of the clauses which he considered contrary to his prerogatives, and had the Magna Carta removed from the church

102. See this page on Pecham. Adam Marsh had been proposed for the see of Ely in 1257, but Rome favored another candidate, Hugh Balsham; see p. 78 and references. St. Bonaventure was chosen Archbishop of York in 1265 by Clement IV (*Cal. Papal Letters,* I, 431) but evidently declined the honor. Peter, Bishop of Corbavia in Dalmatia, was for a time Suffragan Bishop of London, Canterbury and Winchester during the early fourteenth century (Kingsford, *Grey Friars of London,* p. 72), but John Pecham and William of Gainsborough were the only Englishmen to occupy English bishoprics during the period with which we are here dealing.

In Ireland during the same period there were many Franciscan bishops. In 1244 Henry III granted their petition to be allowed to receive bishoprics and archbishoprics (*Cal. Pat., 1232-1247,* p. 444), and thereafter many appointments are recorded (*ibid., 1247-1258,* p. 179; *1272-1281,* pp. 80, 368, 390, 420; *1281-1292,* p. 375; *1301-1307,* pp. 130, 160, etc.). On Germany see Koch, *op. cit.,* pp. 98-9.

103. *Cal. Close, 1272-1279,* p. 232.

104. Hilda Johnstone in *Essays Presented to Thomas Frederick Tout* (Manchester, 1925), p. 173.

105. Writing to Pope Nicholas III shortly after his arrival in England, Pecham reminds the Pope that he had been sent to Canterbury "ut in illa meo ministerio reformarem, quae in eadem ecclesiasticam honestatem viriliter macularunt" (*Register,* R. S., Letter 17, pp. 21-3). He had for a long time refused the appointment (*ibid.,* p. lxiii).

106. *Concilia,* II, 35.

doors,[107] Pecham had substantially the same decrees reënacted by the Lambeth Council two years later in spite of Edward's warning to the assembled clergy.[108] Realizing that the king would be displeased, Pecham wrote him a long letter in defense of what had been done, emphasizing the liberties of the Church and Edward's own duty to submit to law as the foundation of his own reign.[109]

True to the Franciscan training in which he gloried,[110] Pecham used every weapon at his command to establish justice and protect the poor and weak against the rich and strong. He could plead and reason as well as threaten and punish. Bishops, abbots, priors, earls, king and queen — none were spared when they violated justice and charity.[111] Pecham excommunicated the clerks of Edward for refusing obedience, and respectfully but firmly defended his action against the remonstrances of the king.[112] He upheld the king's authority against the rebellious Llewellyn, but nevertheless insisted on negotiating with the Welsh for the sake of peace, even though Edward did not approve.[113] When the negotiations failed and the Welsh were defeated in battle, the archbishop demanded that Edward make good the destruction of church property of which his army had been guilty.[114]

So it was throughout his many relations with the king and queen. Pecham's attitude was always one of due reverence and respect for his sovereigns, modified by the principle that he must obey God rather than men.[115] The king had been severe with the Bishop of Winchester, and Pecham did not hesitate to express his astonishment at the fact and plead with the monarch for

---

107. *Ibid.*, p. 40; *Cal. Close, 1272-1279,* p. 582.
108. *Ibid.*, pp. 50-1; 56-7; *Register,* pp. 235-6.
109. *Register,* pp. 239-44; cf. pp. 249-50.
110. *Ibid.*, pp. lx, 66-8, 214-16.
111. See chap. II, pp. 44-6 and below.
112. *Register,* Letters 149, 151, 152, 154, etc.
113. *Ibid.*, pp. 435 *et seq.*
114. See fuller account in chap. VI, pp. 143 *et seq.*.
115. *Register,* Letter 199, p. 239.

leniency.[116] At the same time he asked the intervention of the queen, "because women are said to be more pitiful and devout than men," and because it had been reported that she was responsible for "making the king severe."[117] At another time Pecham wrote to thank the queen for her consolatory letter and some venison which she had sent him; but these marks of the queen's favor were not allowed to deter him from reminding her in his letter of thanks that he had heard complaints of oppression from the people of Westcliffe, for whom he besought the queen's pity. "Besides this," he continued, "for God's sake, my lady, when you receive land or manor acquired by usury of the Jews, take heed that usury is a mortal sin for those who practise it, those who support it, and those who have a share in it, if they do not return it. And therefore I say to you, my very dear lady, before God and before the court of heaven, that you cannot retain things thus acquired, if you do not make amends to those who have lost them in another way, as much as they are worth more than the principal debt amounts to. . . . I do not believe that you retain in any other manner things thus acquired, but I would wish to know it by your letter so that I can make it known to those who think otherwise." The archbishop concludes his letter by inviting the queen to take advantage of the beautiful chapel he had built at Tenham "more for her comfort than his own."[118] Pecham's admonitions do not seem to have been entirely effective, for three years later, December 13, 1286, he wrote to an old school companion who was close to the queen asking him to remonstrate with her for scandalously acquiring lands extorted from Christians by Jewish usurers.[119]

In a similar manner, when the king appropriated money which was set aside for crusade purposes, Pecham demanded an

---

116. *Ibid.*, pp. 553-4.
117. *Ibid.*, p. 555.
118. *Ibid.*, pp. 619-20.
119. *Ibid.*, pp. 937-8. See chap. III, pp. 68, 69.

explanation,[120] and would not rest contented until the king not only promised to restore the money,[121] but had actually made the restoration after the archbishop had appealed to the Pope as well as to Edward himself.[122] As Pecham complained to the queen about undue exactions from the people of Westcliffe, so he also complained to Edward about exactions from the archbishop's tenants at Newcastle,[123] and otherwise demanded that the king redress wrongs.[124]

Friar William of Gainsborough exemplifies a different phase of Franciscan relations to the king and the state. Like John Pecham, he had been a lecturer at Oxford, minister provincial of the English province, and lecturer at the Roman Curia before becoming a bishop.[125] As minister provincial he "was present at the assembly of Norham in June, 1291, called to consider the question of Scottish succession. . . . In October, 1292, he is at Edward's Scottish parliament at Berwick when the same business is under consideration: his stay is prolonged for he is still there in November. In 1294 he, with a Dominican friar, Hugh of Manchester, is acting as proctor of the king of England in the *parlement* of Paris. In August, 1295, he is at parliament at Westminster, and again in September, 1297. In 1302 he is raised to the see of Worcester and thereafter as bishop attends the king's parliaments."[126]

Attending parliament was not altogether an unusual thing for medieval friars,[127] and it was only one of the many ways in which Friar William served his king and country. In 1295, as

---

120. *Ibid.*, pp. 548-9.
121. *Ibid.*, Letter 438.
122. *Ibid.*, pp. 635-39.
123. *Ibid.*, p. 685.
124. *Ibid.*, pp. 523-4.
125. *Grey Friars in Oxford*, pp. 154-56, 160-62.
126. H. R. Richardson, *Transactions of the Royal Historical Society*, 4th Series, XI, 164-65, with references.
127. Adam Marsh had been required to attend (*Mon. Fran.*, I, 105). Edward I summoned "two or three of the wiser friars" of each order to attend his parliament at Lincoln in 1300 (*Cal. Chancery Warrants, 1244-1326*, p. 121).

one "sworn of the king's council," he was sent with his *confrère,* John de Wilton, to the general chapter of the order of Assisi "on the king's behalf, to explain to them *viva voce* certain affairs that concern the king."[128] In 1299 William represented the king's interests at the general chapter of Lyons, whose favor the king asked for certain members of the order who had served him. These brothers, Edward wrote to the minister general, "are threatened with grievous annoyances and labors for this reason, and he requests them to favor the said brethren out of consideration for him, and to replace them in their accustomed offices and degrees, since he cannot bear with patience that they should be oppressed with vengeance by reason of the favor shown to him, and it would not befit the title of probity of the minister general and his brethren if the king should dissimulate and permit the said brethren to be persecuted by their enemies for their service to him; for whom the king remembers that he requested the minister general and his brethren by his letters on a former occasion, which he has thought fit to be repeated, so that they may recognize from this petition how much he has at heart the peaceful state of the aforesaid brethren. He also requests them to promote to the estate of clergy a lay brother of their order whom Brother William of Gainsborough shall name to them, by whom they are desired to send back their pleasure in this and other matters."[129] It is not clear how these persecuted brethren had served the king, unless perhaps they had somehow taken Edward's part in his controversy with the king of France, and their superiors had punished them for their partisanship.

The following year William was summoned to lecture in Rome, and Edward paid his expenses.[130] At the same time he appointed the friar as one of his "proctors and special envoys . . . to receive and confirm the Pope's declaration of peace and concord

128. *Cal. Close, 1288-1296,* p. 440. Edward also asked the prayers of the chapter (*ibid.,* p. 438).
129. *Cal. Close, 1296-1302,* p. 302.
130. *Grey Friars in Oxford,* p. 161.

between the kings of England and France."[131] Two years later, in June, 1302, William was again called upon to join with other envoys to the Roman court in promoting "certain matters which the king has much at heart."[132] And in September of the same year William and his *confrère,* Hugh of Hertepole, were appointed members of another embassy of the king to Pope Boniface VIII "for the final expedition of the matter of the reëstablishment of peace between him and the king of France . . . and other things that the king has committed to them."[133] This embassy enjoyed plenipotentiary powers;[134] but we know that political jealousies in the end prevented the peace and coöperation between Christian powers which the Pope sought to effect with a view to another crusade to the Holy Land.

The fact that Edward was a stickler for his rights and prerogatives was one of the difficulties, and an illustration of his attitude may be seen at the time of Friar William's appointment to the see of Worcester. As the Pope's bull on this occasion committed to William both the spiritualities and the temporalities of the diocese, Edward considered its acceptance by William a violation of his right to confer the temporalities. Though the friar was a faithful and trusted friend of the king and expressed his willingness to receive the temporalities of the diocese from Edward's hands, he was fined one thousand marks for admitting the bull.[135] Formidable as this may sound, however, it did not imply the loss of the king's friendship. Recognizing the friar's poverty, the king advanced one hundred pounds toward the expenses of his installation,[136] and later remitted the entire fine.[137]

In the meantime William had resumed his diplomatic services to the king. In 1305 he received several summonses to par-

131. *Cal. Pat., 1292-1301,* p. 511. See also p. 543 and *Foedera,* I, 920, 921.
132. *Cal. Close, 1296-1302,* p. 584.
133. *Ibid.,* pp. 600, 601.
134. *Cal. Pat., 1301-1307,* p. 62.
135. *Ibid.,* p. 110 (February 4, 1303).
136. *Grey Friars in Oxford,* p. 161; *Annales monastici,* IV, 556.
137. *Cal. Pat., 1301-1307,* p. 421.

liament,[138] and in October headed a delegation consisting of such prominent persons as Walter, Bishop of Coventry and Lichfield, Henry de Lacy and Hugh the Despenser, to Pope Clement V at Lyons to treat with him "concerning a crusade to the Holy Land, peace with the king of France, and other matters touching the salvation of the king's soul."[139] On March 22, 1307, the king requested William "to come to London on the morrow of Holy Trinity next, to Edward, Prince of Wales, prepared to set out with him for France, as the king, desiring that the peace between the king of France and him, lately treated under a certain form and not yet finally concluded, shall be brought to a happy and prosperous ending, proposes to send Edward to the king of France shortly, as is now ordained and agreed upon, and he considers that the bishop's presence will be very useful to his son in prudently directing such a difficult matter and others that may arise."[140] The "difficult matter" was the claiming for young Edward of the hand of Isabella, King Philip's daughter.[141] This marriage had been long considered,[142] and was strongly encouraged by the Pope as a means of insuring peace between the two realms.[143] In June William went with other envoys to Rome to complete the negotiations.[144] On his return through France the bishop fell ill and died at Beauvais, September 17, 1207, and was buried with the Franciscans there. The fact that almost his entire retinue died at the same time gave rise to a suspicion of poisoning.[145]

---

138. *Cal. Close, 1302-1307,* pp. 337, 342, 345.

139. *Cal. Pat., 1301-1307,* p. 387. Cf. pp. 383, 390, 397, 516; and *Cal. Close, 1302-1307,* pp. 351-53.

140. *Cal. Close, 1302-1307,* p. 530.

141. *Lanercost Chronicle,* pp. 210-11.

142. *Cal. Papal Letters,* I, 576.

143. *Lanercost Chronicle,* p. 206.

144. *Cal. Close, 1302-1307,* p. 508; *Cal. Pat., 1301-1307,* pp. 529, 533; *Foedera,* I, 1017.

145. *Mon. Fran.,* I, 537, 533; *Lanercost Chronicle,* pp. 210-11. It may be that William was returning from another special journey to France; see *Eng. Hist. Review,* XLIV, 278.

Was it an omen of the misfortunes that awaited the unhappy prince whose marriage he had arranged? Edward II succeeded his father to the English throne in 1307 and the next year married Isabella as arranged, though it can hardly be said that the marriage succeeded in bringing the peace negotiations between the two countries "to a happy and prosperous ending." There was no open conflict till 1324, but relations were constantly strained; while the Scots, emboldened by French sympathy and secret support, made destructive invasions into English territory. Factions arose in the land, and the weak and frivolous king was eventually deposed by a French-supported invasion headed by his own queen.

During these troublous times, not unlike those of the earlier Barons' War, the Franciscans, in so far as any political attitude is discernible among them, appear to favor the baronial faction headed by the queen. In the first place, one notices a growing nationalist feeling among the Scottish Franciscans. Though Adam Blunt, guardian of the Roxburgh friary, together with a *confrère,* delivered John Balliol's renunciation of homage to Edward I in 1296,[146] it is evident that the king did not consider the Scottish Franciscans inimical to his policies. During the war which followed, Edward at various times lodged in the Roxburgh and Dumfries friaries and showed many favors to the Scottish Franciscans.[147] He exempted the Franciscans from the oath of loyalty required of all other clergy and religious, and restored to the Franciscan friaries the yearly allowance from the royal treasury which had been granted to them by King Alexander III and John Balliol.[148]

After 1309, however, when the Provincial Council of Scottish Clergy assembled in the Dundee Franciscan church gave its formal adherence to Robert Bruce, the Scottish Franciscans became a

146. *Foedera,* I, 836-37; Walsingham, *Ypodigma Neustriae,* p. 198; Rishanger, *Chron. et annales,* pp. 157-8.

147. M. Bryce, *The Scottish Grey Friars,* I, 19-22.

148. *Ibid.,* pp. 20, 21.

source of annoyance to English kings, and during the Edwardian wars which followed they suffered greatly.[149] Edward II tried to have an English friar made Bishop of St. Andrew's in 1317;[150] and another English Friar Minor, Geoffrey de Aylsham, he sought to make Archbishop of Cashel, Ireland, whence he sent Geoffrey and the minister provincial, Thomas Godman, to stop treasonable practices among the Irish friars — for local patriotism was strong there too.[151] Bruce, on the other hand, was most generous to the Franciscans, favoring them above all the other friars in Scotland.[152] Furthermore, while he showed scant respect to the English Franciscan who in 1317 delivered to him the papal bull on the settlement of the Scottish-English controversy,[153] he delivered up without ransom the body of the young Earl of Gloucester and Hereford after Bannockburn at the request of a Franciscan,[154] and spared the Franciscan friary of Preston from the universal destruction meted out in his raid of 1322.[155] The English on their part were apparently less generous where nationality was concerned, especially after 1329 when the Scottish friars received their own vicar and became independent of the English province. In 1333 Edward had the Scottish Franciscans removed from Berwick in favor of English friars,[156] and in 1335 the English raiders

---

149. *Ibid.*, pp. 23-5; *Lanercost Chronicle,* p. 282.

150. *Ibid.*, p. 24.

151. Fitzmaurice and Little, *Materials for the History of the Franciscan Province of Ireland, 1230-1450,* B. S. F. S., vol. IX (Manchester, 1920), pp. xxiii-xxv. In 1327 Edward also transferred the royal alms given regularly to the friary of Adlon to the friary of Cassele because the English friars at Adlon had been supplanted by Irish friars (*Cal. Close, 1327-1330,* p. 167).

152. *The Scottish Grey Friars,* p. 25.

153. *Foedera,* II, 351. The friar's name was Adam de Neuton. See also *Cal. Papal Letters,* II, 420.

154. *Complete Peerage,* VII, 714; *Dict. National Biography,* IV, 383.

155. *Lanercost Chronicle,* p. 246.

156. *The Scottish Grey Friars,* pp. 33-4. The Lanercost chronicler tells an amusing incident at this time (p. 275): "Note that when the Scottish friars had to leave the convent of Berwick and two English friars were introduced, the Scots prepared a feast for them; and during dinner, while some kept their attention with hospitality and conversation, the others broke open the wardrobe containing books, chalices and vestments, gathered them into silk and other kinds of cloth, and carried them off, saying that they were the gifts of the Lord Earl Patrick," i. e., the ninth Earl of Dunbar.

burned the Franciscan dormitory and schools at Dundee and killed one of the friars.[157]

The Franciscan author of the *Lanercost Chronicle,*[158] in spite of his anti-Scotch bias, has no great respect for Edward II. He records how Edward liked to tinker and play in a manner unbecoming a king;[159] and recognizing the king's incompetence, he sympathizes with the Earl of Carlisle, who was put to death for secretly signing a truce with the Scots.[160] He also thought that John of Brittany's capture by the Scots was a just retribution for his having prevented peace between the two peoples[161]— this in spite of the fact that John was a great friend and benefactor of the Franciscans.[162] On the other hand, he tells how badly Queen Isabella was treated by Edward and the wife of Hugh the Despenser,[163] and speaks of her with respect even when he records her faults.[164] After the success of the unfaithful queen's forces, and the deposition of Edward II in favor of Edward III, it was decided to send representative envoys to the old king imprisoned in Kenilworth Castle to apprise him of his fate. Among these envoys were two bishops, two earls, two barons, two abbots, two priors, two justiciaries, two Dominicans, two Carmelites, etc.; "but at the request of my lady the queen, no Friars Minor were sent, so that they would not be the bearers of such an unpleasant message, because she greatly loved the Minorites."[165] This love for the Franciscans continued to the end. As queen, Isabella had in-

---

157. *Lanercost Chronicle,* p. 282.

158. See *Eng. Hist. Review,* xxxi, 269-79.

159. P. 236.

160. *Ibid.,* pp. 249-51. The earl's Franciscan confessor also justified the action (*ibid., loc. cit.*).

161. *Ibid.,* p. 247.

162. See chap. III, pp. 50, 51; see also *Cal. Papal Letters,* II, 55.

163. *Lanercost Chronicle,* p. 254.

164. *Ibid.,* p. 266, etc.

165. *Ibid.,* p. 258. "Quia Minores multum amabat" might possibly refer to the king, but taken both grammatically and historically, the above reading appears more correct. If the queen had thought merely of sparing the friars because of the king's love for them, she would not have sent the Dominicans, with whom the king was even more friendly than with the Franciscans.

terested herself in the friaries at York and Exeter,[166] and was the greatest benefactor of the Grey Friars' Church in London.[167] As queen mother she stayed in the York friary.[168] When Mortimer was finally captured and put to death, the unhappy queen took the habit of the Poor Clares whom she had also befriended.[169] She continued to have a Franciscan confessor[170] and to show favors to the Franciscans and Poor Clares.[171] In the end she was buried in the friars' London church, and her husband's heart was placed in the bosom of her image.[172]

Though Edward II lodged with the Franciscans at York,[173] had Franciscans as his chaplains,[174] and otherwise gave evidence of his esteem for them,[175] his affections seemed to rest more with the Dominicans. He himself protested his "great affection for the Order of Friars Preachers, for many reasons."[176] Not only did he constantly have a Dominican confessor,[177] but built and endowed the Dominican convent at King's Langley in memory of his murdered favorite, Piers Gaveston.[178] Though they incurred the hatred of the barons for doing so, the Oxford Dominicans had received Piers' body and kept it in their church until the shrine at King's Langley was ready for it.[179] The festivities at the Oxford Black Friars in connection with Gaveston's funeral

---

166. *Cal. Pat., 1313-1317,* pp. 166, 398.

167. See this chap., p. 73.

168. See this chap., p. 72.

169. *Lanercost Chronicle,* p. 266; *Cal. Pat., 1313-1317,* p. 131.

170. See this chap., pp. 75, 77.

171. *Litterae Cantuarienses,* R. S., II, 262-64; *Cal. Close, 1349-1354,* p. 341; *Cal. Pat., 1338-1340,* p. 467; *1345-1348,* p. 125; also Kingsford, *Grey Friars of London,* p. 157.

172. *Grey Friars of London,* p. 74.

173. See this chap., p. 72.

174. *Cal. Pat., 1317-1321,* p. 268.

175. E. g. see *Grey Friars in Oxford,* pp. 18-20; and this chap., pp. 72, 92.

176. Hilda Johnstone, ed., *Letters of Prince Edward of Wales, 1304-1305* (Cambridge, 1931), p. 21; see also pp. xv, l, li, 20, 102, 136.

177. *The Antiquary,* XXII, pp. 119, 159.

178. *Chronicles of the Reigns of Edward I and Edward II,* I, 207; also 271, 273.

179. *Ibid., loc. cit.; Lanercost Chronicle,* p. 222; W. G. D. Fletcher, *The Black Friars of Oxford* (Oxford, 1882), p. 8.

lasted many weeks and were attended by the king and a great number of the nobility.[180] When Edward's trouble with the queen became acute, a Dominican, Thomas Dunheved, went to Rome in an effort to get the king a divorce, but returned to find his royal patron a prisoner. He then, with the aid of three other Dominicans, sought to stir up a rising among the people for their old sovereign, but was himself taken and put in prison, where he died.[181] Later, another Dominican became implicated in the conspiracy against Edward III headed by the Earl of Kent in 1330. He was also condemned to perpetual imprisonment, but later regained the royal favor.[182]

Under Edward III one notices the expansion going on in Franciscan building; and the king approved the many grants which friends made to the friars.[183] He himself continued the alms which his predecessors had always granted for the general and provincial chapters of the Franciscans;[184] enjoyed living with the friars;[185] restored the main window of their London church;[186] took up their defense against aggression;[187] and requested their prayers.[188] But the day when the friars figured prominently in the councils of the realm and the diplomacy of the king had evidently passed. According to Parkinson, the Franciscan Gerard Odo was sent to England in 1332 in an effort on the part of the Pope to make peace between England and Scotland,[189] but even

---

180. *Grey Friars in Oxford,* p. 27, note.

181. *Eng. Hist. Review,* XXXI, 119-24; *Lanercost Chronicle,* pp. 258-9, 265.

182. *Eng. Hist. Review,* XXXIII, 245. A Franciscan, Friar Maurice, on the other hand, evidently took the side of the Earl of Hereford in 1321 and tried to induce the townsmen to surrender the royal stronghold of Bristol (*Cal. Close, 1318-1323,* p. 377).

183. See, e. g., *Cal. Pat., 1334-1338,* pp. 116, 117, 248, 497, etc.

184. *Ibid., 1338-1340,* p. 467.

185. See this chap., p. 72.

186. *Ibid.,* p. 73.

187. *Cal. Pat., 1340-1343,* p. 351; *Cal. Close, 1330-1333,* p. 132.

188. *Cal. Close, 1333-1337,* p. 294.

189. *Collectanea Anglo-Minoritica* (London, 1726), p. 147.

as papal nuncios the friars had become much less frequently used. They would continue to do much good work in the care of souls and in education; and people and sovereigns would continue to cherish them for a long time to come; but the zenith of their influence in public affairs had passed by the early part of the fourteenth century.

V

RELATIONS WITH THE CLERGY AND MONKS

From its very beginning the mendicant movement gave rise to a grave disciplinary problem in the Church. There was no place for these free-lance friars in the traditional ecclesiastical organization. Until the end of the twelfth century the official Church had consistently frowned upon those religious movements which entailed the preaching of the Gospel by laymen.[1] A change of policy took place under Innocent III, and not only were efforts made to win over the heretically inclined Humiliati and Waldenses,[2] but approval was given to the new fraternities of Francis and Dominic. Instead of suppressing the movements, Innocent and his successors determined to direct them. The orthodox elements with proper guidance would steal the thunder of the unorthodox and help to correct the evils to which both groups were more or less opposed.

But papal approval did not remove the dead weight of formalism, the distrust and jealousy on the part of the clergy and older religious orders, which stood in the way of the mendicants. St. Francis' solution to the difficulty of clerical opposition was that of a saint and idealist. He forbade his followers to preach in any diocese whose bishop resented their doing so,[3] or in the parish of any priest who did not welcome them.[4] He even forbade them to have recourse to the Holy See for any kind of privilege or protection against persecutors.[5] Certain brethren, seeing that

1. Grundmann, *Religioese Bewegungen im Mittelalter,* pp. 59 *et seq.*
2. *Ibid.,* pp. 70 *et seq.,* 91, 97 *et seq.*
3. Franciscan Rule, chap. IX; Robinson, *The Writings of St. Francis,* p. 71.
4. Testament of St. Francis, *ibid.,* p. 82.
5. *Ibid.,* p. 84.

bishops sometimes refused them permission to preach, urged Francis to ask the Pope for the privilege of preaching everywhere unmolested. "You friars minor," answered the saint, "do not know the will of God, and will not allow me to convert the whole world as God wills; for I wish first of all by holy humility and reverence to convert the prelates. And when these have seen our holy life and our humble reverence toward them, they will ask you to preach and convert the people, and they will call the people to your sermons better than your privileges, which will lead you to pride. And if you remain free from all covetousness and persuade the people to render the churches their due, they will ask you to hear the confessions of their people; although you should not be concerned about this, for once the people are converted, they will find confessors for themselves."[6]

As the number of the brethren increased, however, and spread over different parts of Christendom, it became evident that they could not carry out their mission without some kind of credentials and even papal protection. The first letter of this nature was issued by Pope Honorius III on June 11, 1219, and addressed to all prelates.[7] Thereafter, many letters of protection and privilege were to follow. In this, as well as in the organization of his order, Francis' idealism was to be modified by the rulers of the Church faced with the alternatives of allowing the fraternity to take its own course and perhaps drift into heresy, or of giving the new order a definite status and somehow fitting it into the existing framework of church organization and discipline. To regret that the Church thus deprived the brotherhood of some of its spontaneity and idealism is only to regret that all the brethren were not St. Francis, or that human nature is not different from what it is. Francis might convert the prelates and

---

6. Paul Sabatier, ed., *Speculum perfectionis* (Paris, 1898), chap. 50, pp. 85-6. See also chap. 54, p. 93 and chap. 87, p. 177.

7. Bull "Cum dilecti," *Bullarium Fran.*, I, 2. It was followed on May 29, 1220, by "Pro dilectis filiis," addressed to the French clergy who still suspected the friars of being heretics (*ibid.*, p. 5; cf. *Chronica Jordani,* no. 4).

clergy by his humility and holiness of life, but his less saintly spiritual sons were soon to find that their help was often least welcome where it was most needed.

Even prelates who were favorably disposed toward the friars sought to restrict their freedom and subject them to a great deal of personal control. Thus in England Roger Niger, Bishop of London from 1229 to 1241, who was an intimate friend of Friar Salomon and "held the order in such reverence that he would rise when any of the brothers greeted him," demanded obedience from them of such a nature that Blessed Agnellus felt justified in applying to the Holy See for protection.[8] The bull *Nimis iniqua,* which was issued in answer to Agnellus' appeal, was addressed to other countries as well as England, and indicates that prelates in France, Germany and elsewhere were also interfering with the unhampered development and activities of the Franciscans by demanding the right to hear the friars' confessions, to bury them, to restrict their number, to collect rents from them, and otherwise subjecting them to their control, even to the extent of appointing their superiors.[9]

As the opposition on the part of the clergy grew, so did the number of papal letters extending the privileges of the friars and defending their rights. It became the policy of the papacy to use the friars as reformers, collectors of crusade money and other revenues, preachers of crusades, and special agents throughout the Christian world and beyond.[10] They were the Pope's centrally controlled shock troops for every emergency, and as such were bound to make enemies, especially as they formed an army

---

8. Eccleston, p. 75.

9. *Bullarium Fran.,* I, 74-6. The bull was issued in August, 1231, and reissued by Innocent IV in July, 1245 (*ibid.,* pp. 368-9, 372-5, 377, etc.), when the Pope appointed bishops in various provinces to act as conservators or protectors of the friars.

10. E. g., Friar William Rubruk and a companion were sent to the Tatars. Golubovich, *Biblioteca,* etc., I, 103, 229-30; also 190-215 on Friar John of Plano Carpini; III, 86-96 on John of Monte Corvino in China and India. Cf. also M. Habig, "Marco Polo's Predecessors," *Catholic World,* August, 1934, pp. 578-85; and "Successors of Marco Polo," *ibid.,* February, 1936, pp. 576-84.

which lived from the territory "invaded," much to the resentment of many ministers of the Gospel to whom their lives and work were a reproach. At the Synod of Cologne in 1239 the legate Conrad heard the complaints of the secular clergy against the invasion of their parishes by the mendicants (in this case especially the Dominicans) who "were reaping in a field not their own." But when one of the objecting pastors admitted that there were no fewer than nine thousand souls in his parish, the legate suspended him from office for his temerity.[11] St. Bonaventure answered the critics of the friars by pointing out that the evil times required their work, and that the seculars were too often both morally and intellectually unfitted for the care of souls, for which reason people were losing confidence in them.[12] He saw the necessity of definitely abandoning St. Francis' idealistic policy for a more realistic one; because, "if our staying depended upon the good-will of the clergy, we should hardly ever dwell in a parish long, for they or others incited by them would drive us out sooner than heretics or Jews."[13]

In England, the opposition to the friars was headed rather by the monks than the seculars. Since so many of the parishes were controlled by monastic institutions, this was as might have been expected. Furthermore, the English bishops, practically without exception friendly to the friars,[14] would hardly have tolerated much opposition on the part of their clergy.[15] The numerous bequests left to the friars on the part of the secular clergy during the thirteenth and succeeding centuries indicates, too, the fairly friendly relations between them.[16] That some of the seculars did object to the friars, however, is indicated by synodal decrees, re-

11. Wadding, *Annales Minorum,* III, 25, 28-9.
12. *Opera omnia,* VIII, 358-378-9.
13. *Ibid.,* p. 365.
14. See chap. II, p. 30 and note.
15. See their instructions to the clergy, chap. II, pp. 26 *et seq.*
16. *Grey Friars in Oxford,* pp. 100 *et seq.; Testa Eboracensia,* Surtees Soc., IV, 24 *et seq.*

ports of visitations, and the like;[17] also by Innocent IV's instructions to English bishops "to restrain all persons from oppressing" the friars in their dioceses.[18] Archbishop Pecham took strong measures against both seculars and monks who withstood the friars' privileges while he acted as their conservator in the province of Canterbury.[19]

The controversy with parish priests was waged around three central problems of jurisdiction and the consequent prestige and emoluments flowing therefrom: namely, preaching, hearing confessions and burying the dead. As pointed out in an earlier chapter, the friars were immediately popular as preachers and confessors. And after they began to have their own cemeteries and larger churches, their places were in demand by prominent persons for burial. All this naturally meant prestige for the friars, and rich and powerful friends and benefactors; which roused the jealousies and, at times, righteous indignation of monks and seculars, who saw their privileges violated, their influence and revenue diminished.[20]

After three-quarters of a century of unpleasantness during which the Popes with few exceptions took the side of the friars, Pope Boniface VIII in 1300 issued the bull *Super cathedram* by

17. See chap. II, pp. 26 *et seq.*, as above; *Concilia,* pp. 133-4, 294, etc.

18. *Cal. Papal Letters,* I, 226; *Bullarium Fran.,* I, 374, 377 (Innocent IV's reissue in 1245 of *Nimis iniqua*).

19. *Register,* pp. 727, 877, and this chapter, below; Little, *Studies,* p. 113. The *Lanercost Chronicle* informs us that when Pope Martin IV issued the bull *Ad fructus uberes* in 1281 (*Bull. Fran.,* III, 480) authorizing the minister general and the minister provincials and definitors to give faculties to the friars, and forbidding anyone to impede the friars in the exercise of them, no less than twenty-one bishops had prohibited the friars from preaching and hearing confessions in their dioceses. It is not stated that there were any English bishops among the twenty-one.

20. St. Bonaventure gives various reasons why the clergy, more than the simple laity, hate the friars and persecute them. First of all, "sicut non omnes laici diligunt nos, sic nec omnes clerici oderunt nos." When they do, it might be for one or more of five reasons: 1) They fear us because we know their faults, etc.; 2) They envy us because we are more pleasing, virtuous, learned, etc.; 3) We learn their secrets from others' confessions; 4) They fear to lose revenue on account of the alms we receive — "et haec videtur potior esse causa pluribus"; 5) It may be God's punishment for their sins. *Opera omnia,* VIII, 355-6. See *ibid.,* p. 374, on why the clergy should love the friars.

which a sort of compromise was reached.[21] Between the issue of this bull and its revocation by Pope Benedict XI three years later,[22] we notice something of a reversal of the old policy of protection, for Boniface commanded the Bishop of Bath and Wells "to protect the rectors and curates of parish churches in the city and diocese of Exeter in their rights, as against the claims and attempts of the Friars Preachers and Minor to infringe upon them by preaching, hearing confessions and burying the dead without their leave."[23] Though entire harmony was never attained and many of the old objections against the friars were to be raised by Richard Fitzralph, Bishop of Armagh, and John Wyclif in the latter part of the century, Pope Boniface's legislation was to form the basis of a fairly acceptable settlement.[24]

The difficulties encountered by the English Franciscans are better illustrated by their relations with the monks. It is by no means an entirely edifying chapter in ecclesiastical history, but it is important for the light it sheds upon the nature and trend of the Franciscan movement and the work done by the friars. With due allowance for the instances of friendly coöperation between monks and friars and for the fact that quarrels and unpleasant scenes have a way of perpetuating themselves while peaceful relations remain unrecorded, one cannot escape the conclusion that the monks bitterly resented the presence and activities of the friars. The monastic chroniclers are virtually unanimous in their condemnation. When they do bestow praise or give recognition, it is usually grudgingly or by implication, as when Matthew Paris tells of their saving the condemned Jews,[25] commends them for returning the alms which the king had stolen to give them,[26] or

---

21. *Bullarium Fran.*, IV, 498.
22. *Ibid.*, V, 2.
23. *Cal. Papal Letters,* I, 608.
24. Little, *Studies,* pp. 114-17. For a more detailed discussion of papal legislation on the pastoral rights and duties of the Franciscans, see M. Bryce, *Scottish Grey Friars,* I, 399-432.
25. *Chron. maj.*, V, 546; see chap. see chap. II, pp. 42, 43.
26. *Chron. maj.*, V, 275-6; see chap. II, p. 46.

admits that because the friars are "vagabonds" they make good messengers through robber-infested countries.[27] Again, while charging the friars with ambition, greed, flattery and generally ulterior motives, he yet admits that the people are everywhere attached to them and that they are responsible for a great harvest of souls.[28] Paris especially bemoans the fact that the monks have had to give way to them for fear of offending important persons.[29]

A notable exception to the usual flow of abuse occurs in the *Gesta abbatum* of Thomas Walsingham. Because the Franciscan Henry of Wodestone had successfully defended the abbot and monks of St. Albans against the Jewish usurers, the chronicler gratefully wrote: "It is indeed quite tenable that God sent His angel to vindicate us. At that very time a Friar Minor called Henry of Wodestone came unexpectedly to our aid, as praiseworthy testimony once came to the help of Holy Susanna . . . and, having examined and fortified our case and destroyed the presumption of our adversaries, he reverently and prudently won the hearts of many to our justice."[30]

But it was not often that the monks had occasion to view a Franciscan as an angel sent by God. The burden of their comments is rather this: "The friars are an upstart band of vagrants; professing humility, yet frequenting the councils and palaces of the great; professing poverty, yet building large monasteries and collecting crusade funds and papal taxes; professing peace, yet stirring up our tenants to discontent; professing meekness, yet appealing to Popes and princes for protection and privileges. These professional beggars have the whole of Christendom by the ears, and flout the customs and conventions which have obtained for centuries. Our orders are hundreds of years old and have shown less disintegration than theirs have in a few decades. Why can we not go on undisturbed in the possession of the pres-

---

27. *Chron. maj.*, IV, 173.
28. *Ibid.*, IV, 279; *Historia Anglorum,* II, 110, 298-9; III, 94, 384, etc.
29. *Chron. maj.*, III, 332-4.
30. *Gesta abbatum,* I, 401-2. See chap. III, pp. 68, 69.

tige we have won by long and honorable service? No good can come of this encroachment upon our revenues and ancient privileges under the pretense of preaching the Gospel to the poor." It was the old order standing out against the new, the lethargic conservatism and formalism of the past entrenched against the new surging of spiritual life and a quickening of the democratic spirit which refused to stand on ceremony or be held in leash by red tape. Taking the monks' point of view, it is small wonder that one of their spokesmen should record with horror under the year 1224: "This same year, O grief, and more than grief! O savage pest, the Friars Minor came to England."[31]

It was not that the monks were always and everywhere hostile to the Franciscans. The monks of Fécamp provided the first friars coming to England with their passage across the channel from France,[32] and the monks of Christ Church, Canterbury, harbored them on their arrival.[33] From 1275 to 1314 the Franciscans provided lecturers for the Canterbury monks and the two communities appear to have got on well together. William of Gainsborough, then minister provincial, wrote to the monks concerning their lector, Friar Ralph of Wydeheye (Wodehay), that though he could be spared with difficulty, and his prudence was much in demand for other work, still, "constrained by the special and sincere affection which I entertain toward you, at your instance, to which I am bound with all my might to accede, I release him for the present with friendly condescension." And in the same spirit, a friar informs us, the monks agreed to the burial of William de Balliol within the ambit of the friars "on account of the sincere devotion which they had toward the order and the brethren of our order from times past." For a century or more these Canterbury monks and friars assisted one another and were able to com-

31. *Peterburgh Chronicle,* edited by J. Sparke in *Historiae Anglicanae Scriptores,* III, 102.

32. Eccleston, pp. 7, 8.

33. *Ibid.,* p. 8.

pose the little differences which occurred over land and rents.[34]

In 1323 the Canterbury monks complained of a certain Friar Salamo de Ripple who was denouncing their prior to the monastic tenants at Sandwich Marsh and claiming that he was responsible for hindering the well-being of the community;[35] but whether Ralph was a Franciscan or a member of one of the other mendicant orders is not clear. Certainly the relations between the Franciscans and monks became definitely strained in 1343, when Isabella, the Queen Dowager, felt called upon to remonstrate with the monks for discontinuing the alms which they had customarily granted the friars. The prior answered that he would be pleased to comply with Isabella's request as soon as the friars ceased to interfere with the collection of rents on monastic lands which they had enclosed.[36] Can it be that this was but a continuation of the trouble caused by Friar Ralph, and that the Franciscans were trying to free the tenants from burdensome rents? In this, as in most other controversies with the monks, we get too little of the friars' side of the story.

At least so much is clear from the above: though "a struggle between friars and monks was inevitable, because they represented different social ideals,"[37] it was not necessarily a violent struggle nor inevitable in the sense that there must be a clash every time the two came together. A little charity and forbearance on both sides was enough to make conditions quite supportable. This conclusion is strengthened by other instances of friendly coöperation. Archbishop Pecham was able to thank the prior and chapter of Coventry for their past benefactions and good-will toward the friars, while pleading with them not to quarrel or prevent the friars from accepting an extension of their holdings from their benefactors.[38] The friars received land from the monks at Shrews-

---

34. C. Cotton, *Collectanea Franciscana,* B. S. F. S., vol. X, pp. 1-8.
35. *Litterae Cantuarienses,* R. S., I, 110.
36. *Ibid.,* II, 262-4.
37. Little, *Studies,* p. 98.
38. *Register,* Letter 698.

bury[39] and Reading,[40] preached in monastic churches,[41] and received monks as members into their order.[42]

The difference in social ideals between monks and friars was indeed marked, as their organizations plainly show. The monastic institutions were strongholds of feudalism. The monks not only held great landed estates cultivated by tenants, but even at times engaged in trade.[43] As a community they were not committed to poverty, and their service to their fellow-men was largely dependent upon the revenues they were able to dispose of by way of charity. It is generally admitted that monastic tenants were better treated than were those of lay lords; but tenants were dependent upon the good-will of the monks for all that, and the relation of serf to landlord was apt to overcast whatever more agreeable relations existed between them. Dr. Little thinks that Abbot John's hostile attitude toward the Franciscans[44] can be explained by the point of view he expresses when he praises the conduct of Simon, Prior of Spalding, who "with his own strength trampled under foot the necks of his proud and rebellious rustics, so that henceforth free men were terrified."[45]

Contrasted with the monks, the Franciscans were bound to poverty even as a community, and in general were faithful to this ideal.[46] Their notion of social service was especially spiritual up-

---

39. *Cal. Chancery Warrants, 1244-1326,* p. 62.

40. *Annales monastici,* III, 134; Eccleston, pp. 99, 100.

41. Owst, *Preaching in Medieval England,* pp. 49-51; *Register* of Archbishop Giffard, Surtees Soc., vol. 109, p. 324; see chap. II, p. 28.

42. See, e. g., *Annales monastici,* III, 133-4; IV, 82; Little, *Grey Friars in Oxford,* pp. 180-81, 235. It must be remarked, however, that this desertion by individuals of one community for another often increased rather than allayed antagonism between the institutions as such. (For an instance of this, see below, pp. 121 *et seq.*). Still, it did indicate that the antagonism was not on a solid and entirely united front.

43. Rose Graham, *English Ecclesiastical Studies* (London, 1929), pp. 263-5; *Cambridge Medieval History,* VI, 484.

44. "Eodem anno, O dolor et plus quam dolor! O pestis truculenta, fratres minores venerunt in Angliam." Abbot John was the Peterburgh chronicler quoted in this chap., p. 105.

45. Little, *Studies,* p. 99, note; *Peterburgh Chronicle,* p. 112: "Superborum rusticorum suorum adversus eum erigentium colla ita propria virtute calcavit, ut ex hoc liberi homines terrerentur."

46. See chap. I, pp. 10-12, 22 *et seq.*

lift and the physical amelioration they could afford by personal attention. To them men were not primarily lords, serfs or tradesmen, but human souls all equally precious in God's sight. They were indeed exponents, in this sense, of the much-abused doctrine of the equality of all men; and this spiritual point of view undoubtedly affected their social outlook as well. But to imagine that the incitement of monastic tenants to revolt against their duly constituted master was a natural deduction from Franciscan social philosophy is no more correct than to hold that Prior Simon's strong-arm methods of repression were a natural deduction from the social philosophy of the monks. Neither case is representative, though they do set forth in exaggerated form the difference in outlook.

True, the friars were charged on more than one occasion with causing disaffection among monastic tenants. The case of Friar Ralph at Sandwich Marsh was not unique. Similar charges were made against the Franciscans at Babwell by the chronicler of St. Edmund's Bury,[47] and by Walsingham in his account of the Peasant Revolt of 1381.[48] In each case we have only the monk's story, without conclusive evidence or clarifying circumstances. Walsingham admits that his charge is based upon conclusions from the general conduct of the friars; and the latter indignantly deny the truth of the accusations.[49] The case against Friar John Gorry of the Dorchester Friary, charged with rousing the tenants of Midleton Abbey during the reign of Richard II, would appear to be better authenticated.[50] But such isolated instances, coming from hostile sources and after the Franciscans had begun to decline, must be appraised in the light of what we know of the friars otherwise. Even if true, they cannot be said to represent Fran-

47. *Memorials of St. Edmund's Abbey,* R. S., II, 335-6.

48. *Historia Anglicana,* R. S., II, 13.

49. Letter of the Oxford mendicants of the four orders to John, Duke of Lancaster, *Fascicula zizaniorum,* R. S., pp. 292-5.

50. A. Réville, *Le soulèvement des travailleurs d'Angleterre en 1381* (Société de l'école des chartes, Paris, 1898), p. lxvii and note.

ciscan teaching. Just as the friars had no thought-out political philosophy, neither had they a system of social philosophy in the modern sense. An intensified practical application of evangelical Christianity, with its insistence on charity, justice and the brotherhood of all men in God — this as taught and interpreted by the Church, and this alone, was the Franciscan social and political philosophy as regards the conduct of the early friars.[51]

It has been pointed out in other places how the writings of the friars support this conclusion.[52] There is no evidence, so far as I know, of any teaching or systematic agitation on their part which looked to the overthrow of the existing order. On the contrary, there is the frank acceptance of the medieval system of society, with its class divisions and the varying grades and conditions of its members. The king and his officials, the clergy, religious, soldiers, doctors and the rest have their place, rights and duties, according to Friar John of Wales;[53] even the humblest laborer is an integral member of the social body and as such is not without honor.[54] Nevertheless, the prince should meditate upon the essential equality of his condition with that of his servant, for he himself is but a servant in relation to God. Hence he must not be proud and lord it over others. The Creator has given us animals to fear us, because it is contrary to nature that man should wish to be feared by his fellows and equals.[55] Those noble by blood should strive to be noble in virtue and not glory in nobility of the flesh, for we are all equally noble in origin. The names freeman and servant arose from ambition and injustice.[56]

---

51. This does not mean that Franciscans, especially of a later date, did not discuss particular aspects of the rights and duties of civil rulers, etc. See R. Scholz, *Unbekannte kirchenpolitische Streitschriften* (Rome, 1911-1914), pp. 167 *et seq.;* 432 *et seq.* Roger Bacon thought the state should maintain the sick and aged. *Opus majus,* edited by Bridges (Oxford, 1897-1900), II, 251.

52. See below, and chap. II, pp. 31 *et seq.;* chap. III, pp. 48-9.

53. *Summa collationum, passim.*

54. *Ibid.,* Pars Prima, Dist. X, Cap. I-IV.

55. *Ibid.,* Pars Secunda, Cap. I.

56. *Ibid.,* Pars Secunda, Dist. III, Cap. I-III.

This was simple Christian doctrine, to recognize the relative positions and dignities of men in society and at the same time the essential equality of all before God, to Whom all must render an account of their stewardship. If Friar Bozon appears to have been particularly severe with tyrannical and covetous lords and prelates, it was only because they were tyrannical and covetous. He condemned the sins of the poor, too, and cautioned them not to seek place and power beyond their status in society.[57] It was precisely because they accepted the principles of a hierarchical society that the popular Franciscan reformers could speak so candidly and severely against the evils which existed within the framework of that society. They were not preaching new truths so much as driving home with a new force the old and partially forgotten truths. If their doctrine hurt in places, or sounded revolutionary, it only showed how sadly needed their enunciation of this doctrine really was. It was revolutionary only in the sense that Christianity itself is revolutionary, or that the encyclicals on labor issued by Popes Leo XIII and Pius XI[58] may appear revolutionary in our secularized and materialistic modern society. As to Matthew Paris' accusation that the friars in their sermons attacked and maligned the monks,[59] we have already called attention to the lack of evidence in support of the charge and to the positive evidence to the contrary.[60]

More galling to the conservative monks than any so-called social philosophy of the friars must have been their reform work in the Church, their employment as papal collectors, and their encroachment upon monastic revenues and prestige. The monks were rightly proud of their past. They had brought the Catholic faith to England centuries before, and under them Christian life and arts had flourished. If they had by the thirteenth century

---

57. *Les contes moralises de Nicole Bozon* (Paris, 1889), Sermons 50 and 75, pp. 68-9, 94-5.

58. *Rerum novarum* and *Quadragesimo anno,* respectively.

59. *Chron. maj.*, IV, 279.

60. See chap. II, pp. 33.

largely given up the care of souls, it was because seculars had come to do the work which the monks were never really intended to do. If they had grown rich in land and revenues, they had worked hard for these things, and they were also severely taxed and at times hard pressed to provide for the beggars and pilgrims whom they never neglected in spite of financial difficulties.[61] Still, there is no denying that some laxity existed among them, and abuses were not uncommon in their administration of the parishes appropriated to their monasteries.[62] Bishop Grosseteste found the monks one of the most formidable obstacles in the path of reform,[63] not so much because of any really great corruption among them, as because of their aloofness and resentment of outside interference.[64] To quote Mr. Stevenson: "Grosseteste's opposition to the monks may, in fact, be summed up as having been occasioned by their lax interpretation and observance of the monastic rule, their reluctance to make proper provision for vicarages, and their disinclination to coöperate with the secular clergy and with the friars in the active work of the diocese. The monks were, in a certain measure, an aristocracy of intellect, and as such looked down upon the ignorance and low standard of the parish priests. They were also, to a considerable extent, an aristocracy of birth, and as such deemed the Franciscans and the Dominicans to be *novi homines,* intruders into a sphere which they regarded as already occupied. It was the existence of feelings and prejudices of that kind which angered Grosseteste. When, on the other hand, the monks adhered strictly to their vows, and led lives of real usefulness, he was to be numbered among their champions and not among their opponents."[65]

---

61. See, e. g., Rose Graham, *English Ecclesiastical Studies,* pp. 100-01, 105, 204-5.

62. See, e. g., *American Historical Review,* July, 1919, pp. 565-77; *Cal. Papal Letters,* I, 150, 303-4, 375; II, 254; *Bullarium Fran.,* I, 689-90; *Episcopal Registers, passim;* also this chapter.

63. Stevenson, *Robert Grosseteste,* pp. 114 *et seq.;* 138 *et seq.*

64. *Ibid.,* pp. 146-63.

65. *Ibid.,* p. 163.

These feelings and prejudices help to explain the difficulties of Grosseteste's helpers, the friars. It could not be expected that the monks would view with equanimity these same friars commissioned by the Pope to investigate their appropriation of parishes, to correct abuses and report them to Rome.[66] More odious still were the friar collectors of papal revenues, men such as Friars John and Mansuetus, who came with authority to summon the monks and command obedience when they were reluctant to comply with demands.[67] Besides, the practical monks had no illusions about the material needs of a community. They had difficulties making ends meet in their own monasteries at times,[68] and the popularity of the begging friars was not calculated to improve their position.

That is why the Benedictines at Reading, when under pressure of the Pope and the king they allotted a building site to the Franciscans in 1233, made such stringent restrictions as to the seeking of alms or new land from the monks and the acceptance by the friars of legacies, tithes or other gifts which might infringe upon the material interests of the abbey.[69] The land given was a low-lying marshy waste near the Thames and only thirty-three by twenty-three perches in size; but even this, according to a monastic chronicler, "was reputed to them [the friars] as a sign of the transgression of evangelical poverty."[70] The first brethren were at all events more than content, and not only agreed to the severe conditions on which the land was allowed them, but at the command of the minister general, Albert of Pisano, returned the deed which guaranteed them undisturbed residence as long as they complied with the conditions.[71] This was in the days when

66. *Cal. Papal Letters,* I, 303-4, 375; *Bulliarum Franciscanum,* I, 689-90.

67. Paris, *Chron. maj.,* IV, 599-600, 617, V, 679.

68. Rose Graham, *English Ecclesiastical Studies,* pp. 100-06, 204-5.

69. *Annales mon.,* III, 134; *Charter Rolls,* July 14, 1233, the deed reprinted in Little; Eccleston, pp. 171-2; J. B. Hurry, *The Reading Abbey* (London, 1901). p. 33.

70. The Dunstable annalist, *Annales mon., loc. cit.*

71. Eccleston, pp. 99, 100.

the friars still burned with zeal for the observance of the ideal of poverty which St. Francis had taught his followers in Italy.

Fifty years later, when experience in a damp, chill northern climate and the problem of providing for large communities had taught the friars a more realistic view of things, they verified the premonitions of the monks by asking for a better site. Archbishop Pecham pleaded with the monks "out of reverence for St. Francis" to extend the property because the friars' grounds were inundated during the wet seasons and the community was subject to grave dangers and inconveniences. The archbishop realized that the first friars had rashly agreed never to seek more land, but believed the Pope had since nullified the contract.[72] Many influential friends took up the cause of the Franciscans, so that the monks finally gave way and granted them a site on higher ground within the town; but with even more stringent safeguards for their own material interests.[73] Some of these restrictions Pecham considered contrary to Franciscan privileges, but hoped to rectify matters in the course of time, if necessary by authority of his position and the royal benevolence. He therefore urged the minister general to give his approval to the deed.[74]

The reasons given by Pecham for demanding a better site afford a fair commentary on the changed attitude gradually assumed by the English Franciscans. "The primitive simplicity of the friars of the English province," he wrote to the minister general, "both in the acquisition of sites and the construction of buildings, being more fervent than prudent, has bequeathed troubles to posterity because, owing to their lack of foresight, it has often become necessary to change the sites and repair the dilapidated buildings."[75] Eccleston had already remarked that the simplicity of the early friars was responsible for their choosing places which could not be enlarged and hence necessitated the acquiring of entirely new

72. *Register,* pp. 414-16.
73. *Ibid.,* Letter 653; *Cal. Close, 1279-88,* p. 428.
74. *Register,* Letter 653.
75. *Ibid., loc. cit.*

sites. He mentions Northampton, Worcester and Hereford as three such places.[76] And Bishop Grosseteste, too, had cautioned the friars against building in low-lying places near the water because they were unhealthy.[77] Later on, the wisdom of this advice was realized when a number of sites proved unsanitary and liable to inundation.[78] At Exeter, for example, the Earl of Hereford, after lodging with the Franciscans there in 1285, reported that the friary was "in a horrible drain, where the place smelled indoors and out, and that within two years nine brothers had died." For this reason the earl approached Edward I and pleaded: "Lord King, for God's sake, request the bishop to provide them with a better place."[79] Under such conditions it was not unnatural that the later friars should come to the conclusion that the simplicity of the first brethren had been "more fervent than prudent." It was certainly proving expensive, now that problems of health, education and increased numbers had become acute. And the monks could well view the material expansion with some alarm.[80]

St. Francis foresaw that property meant cares and struggles. That is why he would have none of it. But St. Francis had in mind a much smaller number of followers fired by his own zeal and detachment.[81] Despite the good work that his spiritual sons were doing in England, he would surely have lamented any conflict with others, the more so if this conflict was over the goods

76. Eccleston, p. 55.

77. *Ibid.,* p. 117.

78. See Little, *Studies,* pp. 10-13.

79. Little and Easterling, *The Franciscans and Dominicans of Exeter* (Exeter, 1927), p. 15. See sequel to the earl's appeal, chap. II, p. 38.

80. See chap. I, p. 19, for St. Bonaventure's reasons why the friars should have larger houses. The saint also argued that it was better to build several stories than bear the cost of a building sufficiently spread out to give the brethren enough fresh air and room for regular observance. Bonaventure, furthermore, preferred stone houses on account of the danger of fire to the friars or their neighbors. Besides, frequent building was expensive, and "non solum corporibus, sed etiam cordibus magna est destructio, nova saepius aedificia construere," especially if there is no other means than begging (*Opera omnia,* VIII, 341). That the fire hazard was real enough in medieval England, see the evidence in Knoop and Jones, *The Medieval Mason* (Manchester, 1933), pp. 6-8.

81. See chap. I, p. 20.

of this world. But for very good reasons the Church had taken the order under her protection and guidance, and knowing that humanly speaking Francis' ideal in its pure form could not endure, had made concessions to the brethren. Under this guidance the friars were able to fill a great need of the age, perhaps in a less ideal way than Francis had in mind; but perhaps too, men being what they are, in the only possible way. The truth of this will become clearer as we review some of the cases of conflict between the English friars and the older monastic institutions.

The struggles which took place at St. Edmund's Bury and at Scarborough are typical if exaggerated instances of the conflicting interests and aspirations of the two groups. According to the Dunstable annalist,[82] the Franciscans tried to settle at St. Edmund's as early as 1233. In 1238 both the Dominicans and the Franciscans are supposed to have petitioned the papal legate Otto for permission to establish houses there;[83] and it was probably to prevent this that the monks that same year obtained the privilege from Pope Gregory IX that no one might build a chapel or convent "within four crosses distant one mile from either side" of St. Edmund's.[84] This did not prevent Pope Alexander IV from allowing the Franciscans to settle in the town in 1257 on condition that a plot of ground be given them by the charity of the faithful.[85] The friars had no difficulty in getting a site,[86] and promptly took advantage of the permission granted them. The monks on their part, however, just as promptly drove them out, "without the injury of violence, but not without ignominy." A papal delegation then investigated the case and restored the friars in a new place to the west of the town. But during the ceremony of induction the monks violently expelled both the delegates and the friars. Next, the friars appealed to the king. Their cause was

---

82. *Annales mon.*, III, 134.
83. *Memorials of St. Edmund's Abbey,* III, 28.
84. *Cal. Papal Letters,* I, 172.
85. *Memorials of St. Edmund's Abbey,* II, 264.
86. *Ibid., loc. cit.;* III, 292; *Monumenta Fran.*, II, 274; *Cal. Pat., 1258-1266,* p. 50 — whence it is clear that several sites were available.

taken up by Queen Eleanor, the Lord Edward and some influential nobles, and in 1258 they were reinstated on the king's own land and granted royal protection.[87]

The following year King Henry wrote to Abbot Simon that "he will remember that in the forty-second year [i. e., 1258] the king sent Gilbert de Preston, justice, to establish the Friars Minor in the town of St. Edmund's on the king's farm, given to him by Lewis de Gerardivilla and Pernell his wife, and the king knew that the abbot and convent had already received an apostolic mandate to receive them kindly. Now, the king informs him that, having had a deliberation of the council, he by the consent and approval of his sworn counselors has ratified the said act, and wishes it to be promoted to a prosperous conclusion and to be maintained by the king and his heirs, and he will cause any persons who put any impediment in the way of the said friars to be punished. Therefore he requests and requires the abbot to cherish and protect the friars and show kindness to their benefactors, that he may obtain the blessing of God and the king's favor."[88] Still, the monks did not give up the fight. Finding the next Pope, Urban IV, more favorable to them, they persuaded him to order the friars to leave their buildings and destroy them. In the end, as the monastic chronicler admits, the friars obeyed humbly, publicly confessing their fault before the clergy and people assembled in the basilica.[89]

But the victorious monks had yet another force to reckon with. The people began to murmur so ominously against their treatment of the friars that it was decided to allow them to settle outside the town at Babwell.[90] Pope Alexander IV had been persuaded

87. *Memorials,* II, 265 *et seq.;* Paris, *Chron. maj.,* V, 688; *Cal. Pat., 1258-1266,* p. 50.

88. *Cal. Pat., 1258-1266,* p. 50. Similar letters were sent to the prior and convent of St. Edmund's and to the aldermen, bailiffs and "good men" of the town. Reprinted in *Memorials, loc. cit.*

89. *Memorials,* II, 269; III, 30.

90. *Ibid., loc. cit.* Cf. also on St. Edmund's case, Dugdale, *Monasticon* (London, 1821), III, 106-7.

that the presence of the Franciscans at St. Edmund's was for the good of souls,[91] and there can be little doubt that it was. As elsewhere, the people welcomed their ministrations, and therefore greatly resented their removal. This naturally prepared the way for the later accusations that the Franciscans instigated and abetted the riots of 1326-1327 against the monks.[92] If the chronicler's account can be relied upon, the secular clergy actually led the rioters, with the friars as their allies,[93] a combination not without significance of the resentment in some quarters against evils in the system of parish appropriation and monastic administration. It was against these evils that Grosseteste had fought as tending to keep down the standard of clerical efficiency to the detriment of souls.[94] This was not the first trouble the monks of St. Edmund had with the burghers of the town. Abbot Samson had granted them a charter in answer to their demands in 1292,[95] and from the terms of settlement it appears that the liberties of the town were one of the points of contention also in the present instance.[96] In view of this trend, perhaps it was well that the friars at least retained the confidence of the townsmen, so as to temper their discontent with Christian principles.

At Scarborough the Franciscans had settled before 1240.[97] Since their place was within the jurisdiction of St. Mary's Church, appropriated to the Cistercians at Citeaux, the monks protested against their presence. Bishop Grosseteste received a papal order to investigate, and if he found that the charges of the monks were true, to have the friars banished and their buildings destroyed.[98] The friars at first urged a papal privilege against being summoned by Grosseteste, then submitted to the investigation and contested

91. *Ibid.,* p. 281.
92. *Ibid.,* III, 335-61.
93. *Ibid.,* pp. 335-6.
94. Stevenson, *Robert Grosseteste,* pp. 138-46.
95. *Memorials* (Jocelin de Brakeland's Chronicle), pp. 279-81, 299-304.
96. *Memorials,* III, 357-61.
97. The king ordered the sheriff of York to provide the friars with food and clothing, February 5, 1239-1240; *Liberate Rolls, 1226-1240,* p. 447.
98. See account in *Victoria County Histories,* Yorks., III, 274.

the effort to dismiss them. On the third day of the proceedings, however, a spokesman of the friars expressed willingness to withdraw peacefully, though he maintained that they might justifiably resist the monks, since here was a case of contending not for property rights, but for "the salvation of souls accruing from their dwelling in the said place." And he quoted Scripture to prove that in such a case "ordinary law and rights must give way to the salvation of souls." With this he begged pardon for the friars on bended knees, and declared they would leave as the more Franciscan thing to do.[99]

But again there was the attachment of the people to consider, and Grosseteste reminded the monks that the dismissal of the friars "would not redound to the honor of your order, but rather blacken the splendor of its reputation and put a considerable blot upon its glory." Therefore, he asked them to reconsider their decision.[100] The matter was referred to the Abbot of Citeaux, who decided that the friars must go;[101] and in August, 1245, Henry III granted the banished brethren a new site and ordered the bailiffs to help them to remove their church.[102]

Still the trouble was not ended. Some time between 1267 and 1272 the Franciscans returned to Scarborough,[103] and in 1281 the Abbot of St. Albans, conservator of the privileges of the Cistercians, again ordered them to leave, under pain of excommunication on all who celebrated in their church or attended their services. But the friars now had a determined champion in Archbishop Pecham. After requesting in vain that time be given to the Bishop of Worcester, specially appointed conservator of the friars, to examine the case, the archbishop declared the excommunication null and void. He maintained that the Abbot of St.

---

99. *R. Grosseteste epistolae,* pp. 321-3. For privilege of not being summoned, see *Bullarium Fran.,* I, 184, bull *Cum jam per* issued by Gregory IX, 1236; reissued in 1243 and 1244. *Ibid.,* pp. 318, 347.

100. *Grosseteste epistolae, loc. cit.*

101. *Victoria County Histories,* Yorks., III, 274-5.

102. *Cal. Pat., 1232-1247,* p. 459; *Close Rolls, 1242-1247,* p. 334.

103. *Victoria County Histories,* Yorks., III, 275.

Albans had no jurisdiction over the friars, who had a papal license "to build churches and oratories wherever it seems to them expedient,"[104] and urged the proctor of the Franciscans in Rome to resist the oppression of these "demoniac monks" because the honor of the order was at stake.[105] Pecham believed, too, that the friars' presence in Scarborough was for the salvation of souls,[106] and that they were encountering the opposition of the "enemies of Christ."[107] Hence he was determined not to give way. Adam Marsh had felt pretty much the same about the first encounter at Scarborough, though his attitude was more conciliatory and resigned.[108]

Bishop Giffard of Worcester appealed in behalf of the Scarborough friars in 1281,[109] and three years later Archbishop Wickwane severely rebuked the Cistercians for resisting these "most religious men"; demanding that in future they be allowed to preach and hold services at suitable hours and places for the accommodation of the people.[110] Again we hear the argument that the good of souls was at stake. Referring to the statement in St. Paul's Letter to the Romans, X, 17, that "faith . . . cometh by hearing," the archbishop reminded the monks that those who hinder preaching hinder faith.[111] But the prelate's preaching was wasted on the monks, for the Cistercian general chapter of 1285 appealed to Edward I against the Franciscans and Dominicans at Scarborough, stating that their presence there was contrary to royal and papal privileges of the monks, and complaining bitterly of the decline in their income because of the friars.[112] Though there was apparently still some difficulty over the matter of hearing

---

104. Pecham's *Register,* Letters 181-2, pp. 214 *et seq.;* Letters 202-3, pp. 246-9; Letter 228, pp. 284-5.
105. *Ibid.,* pp. 284-5.
106. *Ibid.,* p. 215.
107. *Ibid.,* p. 246.
108. *Mon. Fran.,* I, 406.
109. Pecham's *Register,* p. 216; Giffard's *Register,* Worcester Hist. Soc., p. 135.
110. *Historical Papers and Letters from the Northern Registers,* p. 79.
111. *Ibid., loc. cit.*
112. *Foedera,* I, 661.

confessions in 1293,[113] the friars remained in Scarborough. Pope Nicholas IV, in 1290, granted special indulgences to those who visited their church on certain feasts,[114] and in 1291 Archbishop Romanus called on them to preach the crusade.[115]

The regrettable thing is that the Franciscans could not always advance "the salvation of souls" in justification of their conduct. At Worcester and at Gloucester they quarreled with the monks over the right to bury bodies, and Archbishop Pecham championed their claims.[116] However much the friars might have suffered at the hands of the monks, and however right they might have been in point of strict justice, such a quarrel as that at Worcester in 1289 was hardly a credit to the professed followers of St. Francis. Still, in taking up the cause of the friars Pecham must have felt that to give way to the monks in this case was only to provoke further interference with the life and work of the friars. He was thoroughly convinced of the need of the friars, and was not the man to submit meekly to what he considered reactionary persecution of the "enemies of Christ."[117] The people were faced with spiritual starvation; the monks not only refused to feed them, but expelled those who wished to do so. Even if this dog-in-the-manger attitude did not apply in every case, to Pecham it appeared that any weak surrender of rights or privileges to the monks was only making the friars' position the more impossible. If the monks of Worcester could with impunity forcefully carry away a body which the friars had been granted for burial, they could go further and make conditions quite insupportable for them. If the friars, on the other hand, took advantage of Pecham's

113. *Historical Papers and Letters from the Northern Registers,* pp. 102-3.

114. *Cal. Papal Letters,* I, 521.

115. *Historical Papers and Letters from the Northern Registers,* p. 95.

116. *Annales mon.,* IV, 499-504; Pecham's *Register,* p. 905.

117. The monks, as Pecham's *Register* shows, gave him much trouble as archbishop and there was reason often for his severity with them. At other times he could be very friendly. Pecham's interference with the foundation of Gloucester College, Oxford, showed that he had his own notions as to what monks should be. *Register,* pp. 150-51; *Transactions of the Royal Historical Society,* 4th Series, X, 210-11.

interference in their behalf and carried back the body in boisterous triumph, as the monastic chronicler alleges,[118] it was far from becoming their spiritual ancestry, even though the provocation to such conduct was great enough to explain it. On the Franciscan side we have merely the statement by an anonymous chronicler that the body of Henry Poche, which had been taken by the monks "with injury and violence," was returned to the friars.[119]

In the earlier days there was probably many a similar case settled by Franciscan meekness. Now, with two Franciscans, Pope Nicholas IV and Archbishop Pecham, to champion their rights, they begin to emerge as less lovable fighters.[120] Pecham seemed especially determined to break the opposition of the monks. The case of William of Pershore, of which we have unusually complete records, may be cited as a final illustration of the rivalry between the new and the old orders in the Church.

William had left the Benedictines to become a Franciscan. In 1290 he apostatized and fled from the Franciscan convent with books belonging to the friars. Archbishop Pecham applied a privilege possessed by the Franciscans and published an excommunication against William and all who harbored him. It so happened that William had taken refuge with the monks of Westminster, who refused to give him up and eventually allowed him to escape. The case was taken to Rome and a papal court returned a verdict wholly in favor of the friars. Among other things, the monks were obliged to help to recover the fugitive, restore the stolen books, seek reconciliation with the Franciscans, and pay a substantial fine to cover the losses sustained by the friars. After prolonged litigation, the friars in the interest of peace offered to accept a much smaller sum of money, to be paid to their needy

---

118. *Annales mon., loc. cit.*

119. *Victoria County Histories,* Worcesters., II, 170.

120. The chronicler of Westminster (*Flores historiarum,* R. S., III, 75), refers to Nicholas as the sun and Pecham as the moon, under whom the friars began to "raise up their horns throughout the world, sparing no order or reputation in the English province."

friaries at Winchelsea and Lichfield, and to turn over all documents relating to the case as soon as payment was made. On these modified terms harmony was finally restored just before Christmas, 1294.[121]

Again the Franciscans had defended their rights instead of practising the meek submission taught by St. Francis. But too much has been made of this fact as evidencing the utter decline of the Franciscans. Particularly strange is the argumentation of Mr. Howlett, who admits that the Franciscans "seem to have been in the right all through," and allows that it was "creditable" in them to have subsequently modified the terms of settlement as a pacific and brotherly gesture, and yet is able to continue as follows: "A complete triumph like this over the wealthiest abbot of the great Benedictine order is somewhat of a Pyrrhic victory after all. There is a moral loss in a contest which would assuredly have been instantly abandoned as unworthy a Minorite, we will not say by St. Francis or even Agnellus of Pisa, but by Haymo of Faversham, a man who could fight a stout fight for his rule within the order. Such a victory, too, over one of their admitted chiefs must at once have increased the growing bitterness against the Minorites. The enmity, moreover, of these particular monks of Westminster cannot be accounted a light thing to encounter, for these, or many of them, were the men who appear in the Patent Roll of 31 Edward [*Cal. Pat., 1301-1307,* pp. 194-5] as having been consigned to the tower for the celebrated robbery of the King's treasury in 1303. One of them, Alexander of Pershore, prominent as proctor at Rome against the Franciscans, was certainly the man who took the black panniers full of treasure to the pier, and who threatened to kill John Albon if he revealed the crime."[122]

---

121. *Mon. Fran.,* II, 31-62, where all the documents relating to the case are printed.

122. *Mon. Fran.,* II, xv-xvi. On the story of the robbery, see T. F. Tout *Chapters in the Administrative History of Medieval England* (Manchester, 1920), II, 55-58, and references.

Mr. Howlett's quite admissible opinion that the contest was unworthy of a Franciscan is, to say the least, not supported by his introduction of Alexander of Pershore and his fellows in crime. If such had been the character of the monks in every contest with the friars, Pecham would have been quite justified in referring to them as "demoniac monks" and "enemies of Christ"; and I am not so sure that Blessed Agnellus, who applied for papal protection of Franciscan liberties against a friendly bishop,[123] would have tamely allowed the monks to harbor one who could do so much damage to the order and religion by being at large. Mr. Kingsford rightly remarks that a few vagabond friars probably did more harm to the reputation of the friars than was deserved;[124] and the civil authorities of the time sufficiently realized the harm done by these public enemies to give every assistance in their arrest.[125] Especially about the beginning of the fourteenth century the evil seems to have grown. Other orders besides the Franciscans were having trouble with apostates, some apostate Dominicans going so far as to engage in defamatory writings and to appoint their own proctor.[126]

It is easy to charge the Franciscans with infidelity to their profession just because their chosen standard was so very high. Thus Matthew Paris would have us believe that all who heard of their forced entry into St. Edmund's "could not sufficiently wonder that such holy men who had chosen voluntary poverty" could be guilty of violating the privileges of the abbey.[127] And the chronicler of St. Edmund's was shocked that such "religious and venerable men," who professed to follow the Gospel counsels and the meek St. Francis, should resist expulsion and appeal to authority for protection. St. Francis, he thought, was "probably

---

123. See this chap., p. 100.

124. *The Grey Friars of London,* p. 19.

125. See chap. I, p. 20, and references below.

126. *Cal. Pat., 1313-1317,* pp. 176, 186; also *1301-1307,* p. 123; *1307-1313,* pp. 141, 182; *1313-1317,* pp. 177, 217, 512, etc.

127. *Chron. maj.,* V, 688.

asleep."[128] The retort is not merely that St. Benedict also appeared to nap occasionally; but that the friars did, as far as we know, at least refrain from violence, and they were usually the first to seek pardon and reconciliation, whether the decision of authority was for or against them. Though the conduct and motives of the friars were attacked from the very beginning of their English apostolate, the evidence in general points to their great influence for good and the zeal for souls which actuated them.

The bishops everywhere welcomed them for the good they did. Bishop Grosseteste remarked not only "the inestimable benefits accruing to our people" through the friars, but the "advance" made by seculars and regulars through imitation of them.[129] The friars helped the clergy by their sermon materials and treatises on confession, and by their schools of theology.[130] They also lectured to the monks, and were responsible for raising the tone of learning and living throughout the land.[131] Mr. Howlett's contention that they "destroyed the possibility of that natural balance which years would assuredly have brought about between seculars and regulars, and thus, in the great result, lost to the Papacy a kingdom destined to be of primary importance in Europe"[132] is in keeping with his peace-at-any-price attitude regarding their relations with the monks of Westminster. Reform and instruction of the clergy and masses were needed in the Church. What the friars did in this respect more than made up for the accidental scandals which arose out of their differences with those who resisted them mostly out of jealousy and selfishness.

Nor is it quite fair to hold that, as a consequence of their centralized government, the friars of the English province as a whole were responsible for the quarrels which took place, where-

---

128. *Memorials of St. Edmund's Abbey,* III, 264-7.
129. See chap. II, pp. 26 *et seq.*
130. See chap. VI; Little, *Studies,* pp. 119, 157 *et seq.;* 173 *et seq.*
131. This chap., p. 105; chap. VI, pp. 127-133.
132. *Mon. Fran.,* II, ix.

as with the monks only individual houses were responsible.[133] In spite of their centralized government, the Franciscans were highly individualistic and had great freedom of movement. Particular members of the order, or particular houses might easily be guilty of offenses not approved by the province as such. Besides, the Benedictine and Cistercian houses were not unconnected,[134] and we find Archbishop Pecham writing to the Abbot of Chertsey, president of the Benedictine chapter, demanding the release of William of Pershore,[135] and to the Abingdon monks forbidding them to receive him.[136] In the Scarborough case, as we have seen, the Abbot of Citeaux and the whole Cistercian chapter were involved.[137] There is no need of painting one group black in order to save the reputation of the other. Both had their faults, both had their unworthy members, both were human and naturally differed in their points of view.

---

133. Howlett, *Mon. Fran.*, II, xiii; Sever, *English Franciscans under Henry III* (Oxford, 1915), p. 105.
134. See *Transactions of the Royal Historical Society,* 4th Series, X, 195-263; and note 137, below.
135. *Register,* Letter 709.
136. *Ibid.,* Letter 706.
137. See this chap., pp. 118, 119.

VI

ALL THINGS TO ALL MEN

The device of treating medieval Franciscans in their relations to various classes of society has its obvious defects. The very difficulties and repetitions involved in so doing emphasize the classless nature of the Franciscan movement. Like the Church, which the friars sought to revitalize and to which they professed unswerving loyalty, the Franciscan movement was in a very real sense all-embracing. Its greatest charm and the secret of its phenomenal success lay precisely in the catholicity of its appeal, whether we spell catholicity with a small or a large initial letter. Because the friars preached Christianity by word and example to all without distinction, all classes trusted them. Because for a long time they were able to keep aloof from the worst features of nationalism and local patriotism, they were a bond of unity between the nations as well as between classes within the nations. Because they represented the best Christian thought and sentiment of their age, and did not hesitate to test and apply the theories of the schools in the laboratory of daily life and work, they were progressive men and equal to every task. Who better fitted to guide and instruct others than those who lived the doctrine they preached? Who better fitted to preach the crusades which appealed so much to medieval Christian piety than those who themselves went to the Holy Land as crusaders and missionaries? Who better fitted to make peace between quarreling princes and townsmen than those who accepted all men as brothers and recognized no racial, national or class boundaries in their pursuit of souls? Who better able than such men to unite all in a common allegiance to the Church and its head in Rome?

Franciscan activities cut across social and territorial groupings and made the friars at once a leaven and a unifying element in society as a whole. Learning or education was one such activity in which the English Franciscans greatly excelled. We might devote a special chapter to the relations between friars and scholars, or discuss in some detail the academic attainments of the friars and the organization which made these possible; but these subjects require lengthier treatment than is possible here. For the present we are interested in Franciscan educational activities viewed rather as a means of influence and uplift among the people and their leaders than as a contribution to the speculative thought of the age.[1]

Though the English friars were early looked upon as *viri litterati*[2] and great promoters of learning by such an antagonist as Matthew Paris, who tells us that the Cistercians were driven to open a school at Paris "so that they would no longer be an object of contempt with the Friars Preachers and Minor and learned seculars,"[3] we must bear in mind that the Franciscans were first and foremost practical men, men of action. Education for them was primarily a training for the apostolate; and in this sense St. Francis, for all his distrust of learning, approved of study among his followers.[4] Friar John of Wales states the Franciscan attitude toward learning when he writes: "This is the fruit of true philosophy, to know how to speak orderly, decently and usefully with

---

1. For fuller treatment of the medieval Franciscans as scholars and educators see Hilarin Felder, *Geschichte der wissenschaftlichen Studien im Franciskanerorden,* etc. (Freiburg, 1904); D. E. Sharp, *Franciscan Philosophy at Oxford* (Oxford, 1930); Little and Pelster, *Oxford Theology and Theologians* (Oxford, 1934); A. G. Little, "The Franciscan School at Oxford in the Thirteenth Century," *Archivum Fran. hist.* (Quaracchi, 1926), XIX, 803-874; A. G. Little, "The Educational Organization of the Mendicant Friars in England," *Trans. Royal Hist. Soc.,* New Series, VIII, 49-70; *Studies in English Franciscan History,* pp. 193-221; J. H. Bridges, *Life and Work of Roger Bacon* (London, 1914); *The Grey Friars in Oxford, passim;* etc.

2. Paris, *Chron. maj.,* IV, 9.

3. Paris, *Chron. maj.,* V, 79; *Hist. Anglorum,* II, 110, 298-9, etc.

4. Felder, *Geschichte der wissenschaftlichen Studien,* pp. 58, 64 *et seq.*

men of all ranks, ages, positions, duties and offices; namely, to know how to speak with kings as is becoming, and thus with the rest."[5] Learning is not to be sought for its own sake, out of vain-glory or curiosity, nor for the sake of honors and gain, but for the edification of oneself and others.[6] Roger Bacon maintained that preaching was the principal intention and final end of the Church;[7] and preaching was the goal of theological studies among the friars,[8] while all other sciences were the handmaids of theology.[9]

The Spirituals in the order might lament with Jacopone da Todi that "Paris has destroyed Assisi,"[10] and a character like William Ockham might be instanced as exemplifying St. Francis' fears of the learning which puffs up; but after we have heard all the objections, we cannot but commend the wisdom of Bishop Grosseteste, who told the English Franciscans that "unless they fostered study and studiously devoted themselves to the divine law, it would happen with them, as with other religious whom we see, O grief! walking in the darkness of ignorance."[11] Far from undermining religious observance and spirituality, as the Spirituals feared, study may well have prevented the friars from declining sooner than they did. St. Bonaventure recognized the value of study in personal sanctification;[12] and it is significant that the most enthusiastic cultivation of learning in the order was contemporaneous, to a great extent, with the most zealous cultiva-

---

5. *Summa collationum,* Prologue.
6. *Ibid.,* Pars Quinta, Dist. II, Cap. III.
7. *Opus minus* (*Opera adhuc inedita,* R. S.), p. 323.
8. Felder, *op. cit.,* pp. 349 *et seq.*
9. Little, *Studies,* pp. 206-7. St. Bonaventure, *Opera omnia,* VIII, 339, explained that the friars put much time on study because of its necessity for preaching, hearing confessions and expounding the Scriptures. The study of Scripture was useful for one's own instruction and guidance as well as for the instruction of others. Paul had exhorted Timothy to read the Scriptures, etc.
10. "Mal vedemmo Parisi,
    Ch'n'ha destrutto Ascisi;
    Con la lor lettoria
    L'han messo in mala via."
    —Quoted by Felder, *op. cit.,* p. 379.
11. Eccleston, p. 114.
12. See note 9 above.

tion of the spiritual life. The English province before Eccleston's time was famous for both study and virtue.[13] Certainly, the success of the friars in various fields of the apostolate was due in no small measure to their pursuit of learning. The two went hand in hand, as Matthew Paris observed on several occasions.[14]

Such outstanding public figures as Adam Marsh, Haymo of Faversham, John of Wales, John Pecham and William of Gainsborough were university men, as were Adam of Oxford, missionary to the Orient, and William of Heddele, who accompanied Edward I to the Holy Land.[15] Eccleston assures us that the flocking of learned men to the order increased the prestige of the brethren,[16] and that with the establishment of the school at Oxford the friars very soon made strides in the art of preaching.[17] They were much in demand as confessors;[18] and it is Dr. Little's opinion that, owing to the lack of training among the parish clergy, auricular confession as made compulsory in the Lateran Council of 1215 would never have been enforced without the friars.[19] Roger Bacon urged the study of oriental languages both as a means of access to the original texts in theology, philosophy and science, and for the practical purpose of preaching to the in-

---

13. Eccleston, pp. 62, 86, 89, 98-9.

14. *Chron. maj.,* IV, p. 9. The friars and other learned men handled the business of the crusades.

Hist. Anglorum, II, 110: "Tandem scolas theologicae infra septa sua constituentes, legentes et disputantes, at populo praedicantes, fructum horrea Christi, quia messis multa et operarii pauci fuerant, non modicum reportarunt."

Ibid., II, 298-9: "Officio praedicationis, studii et eruditionis strenue intenderunt, et ad eorum ordinem nobiles, clerici et etiam praelati coeperunt convolare. Multi autem ex eis ad regimen nobilium ecclesiarum cathedralium rite electi, fructum in ecclesia Dei verbo et opere multiplicantes, feliciter floruerunt." See also *ibid.,* III, 94, 384, etc.

15. *Grey Friars in Oxford,* pp. 134-62, 178-9.

16. Eccleston, pp. 20 *et seq.*

17. *Ibid.,* pp. 60, 61.

18. See chap. II, pp. 29 *et seq.*

19. *Studies,* p. 120. Dr. Little's statement that "auricular confession only became general and compulsory after the Lateran Council" is open to misunderstanding. The Fourth Lateran Council made *annual* auricular confession of obligation. Hefele's *Histoire des conciles* (Paris, 1913), vol. V, Can. 21, pp. 1349-51. Friar Bozon urged his hearers to confess three times annually; *Les contes moralises,* Sermon 106. The same was urged by various English synods; *Concilia,* pp. 133, 294, etc.

fidels.[20] He himself composed grammars in Greek and Hebrew to facilitate such studies.[21] The works of men like John of Wales, John Pecham, Bartholomew the Englishman and others show the practical trend of Franciscan learning.[22] Helps to preachers and confessors, Scriptural commentaries, sermon materials, instructions on the vices and virtues, helps to Christian living — these are the kinds of treatises which predominate. The widely-used *De proprietatibus rerum* of Friar Bartholomew was a sort of encyclopedia of all the learning of his day collected, as the friar himself tells us, to help simple Christians like himself "to understand the enigmas of Scripture which are hidden under the symbols and figures of the properties of natural and artificial things."[23] It was especially dedicated to future preachers of the order.[24] To understand and preach the Scriptures, one must have correct knowledge of the things of which they speak. This was the Franciscan justification of scientific studies.[25]

Bishop Grosseteste, first lector to the English Franciscans at Oxford,[26] and the man who more than any other was responsible for turning the friars toward learning, was himself a practical man and held that the care of souls was more important than teaching.[27] And it was "the practical bent of his teaching which tended most . . . to create a close bond of union between him and the early Franciscans."[28] Writing to the minister general, Brother

---

20. Bridges, ed., *Opus majus,* III, 115, 119-22.

21. Nolan and Hirsch, *The Greek Grammar of Roger Bacon and a Fragment of His Hebrew Grammar* (Cambridge, 1902), pp. xiii *et seq.,* 199-201, etc.

22. See chap. II, pp. 31 *et seq.; Grey Friars in Oxford,* pp. 143 *et seq.,* 154-6; and notes below.

23. *De proprietatibus rerum* (edn. Nuremburg, 1519), "Prohemium" and "Conclusio libri."

24. See Father Thomas Plassmann's excellent article on Bartholomew, identifying him and describing his work, in *Archivum Franciscanum historicum,* XII, 68-109. See also Felder, *op. cit.,* pp. 248 *et seq.,* 395-6; and Robert Steele, *Medieval Lore* (London, 1893), for enlightening comments on Bartholomew's influence on preaching and literature. *Medieval Lore* is an edition by Steele of Prof. William Morris' translation of parts of Bartholomew's interesting work.

25. *Archivum Franciscanum historicum,* XII, 92, 98, 106-7.

26. Eccleston, p. 60.

27. Stevenson, *Robert Grosseteste,* p. 121.

28. *Ibid.,* p. 37.

Elias, Grosseteste admitted that he loved the Franciscans more than all others, because "in preaching the word of God, hearing confessions, imposing penances, we know of no such efficient helpers in these and similar things as your friars."[29] Under the guiding genius of this great bishop, the friars brought the spirit and benefits of learning to the people and the spirit and benefits of religion to the university. It is not to be wondered at that Grosseteste was devoted to the friars. As they were one with him in his efforts to reform Church and State, so too they were one with him in his efforts to combine the revival of learning with the revival of religion. To this end he fostered the Franciscans, and as Mr. Stevenson points out, his trust and foresight were amply justified; for "nowhere has the Franciscan order done so much as in England for the advancement and dissemination of knowledge, nowhere has it furnished so long a list of distinguished names, and nowhere has it presented so clean a record of useful work. With few exceptions every really great man of learning belonging to the order came from these islands."[30]

These things are not surprising when we realize with what enthusiasm the friars turned to study,[31] so that by the middle of the thirteenth century there were between thirty and forty qualified lectors in the province, and schools were flourishing at Oxford, Cambridge, London, Canterbury, Bristol, Hereford, Leicester, Norwich, and perhaps other places not recorded; while

---

29. *R. Grosseteste epistolae,* pp. 133-4.

30. *Robert Grosseteste,* p. 75. See also Brewer's preface to *Monumenta Fran.,* I, lxxx *et seq.*

In the matter of scholars among the English Franciscans, Father Hilarin Felder points out that Englishmen were the first lectors to the friars in Germany; they were also lectors at Bologna, Padua, Genoa, Rome, Tours, Lyons and Paris. "Thus without a doubt during the first half of the thirteenth century no Franciscan province could compare with the English province in regard to learning. This astounding beginning promised well for the decades and centuries to follow. The English nation has given to the Franciscan Order a greater number of outstanding scholars than all the other nations put together. Indeed, if we glance over the real leaders of Franciscan schools, all, with the exception of St. Bonaventure, were Englishmen" (*op. cit.,* p. 316).

31. See Eccleston, pp. 42-3, 60 *et seq.*

provision was made to keep up the supply of trained teachers by selecting men from the various houses to study at the universities.[32] Most of these attended Oxford or Cambridge, but some were sent to Paris.[33] In 1336 Oxford and Cambridge were the "general" studies of the province; London, York, Norwich, Newcastle-on-Tyne, Stamford, Coventry and Exeter were the "special" studies distributed according to the seven custodies.[34]

By this system the friars were able to give their own men the best possible training, supply lectors for schools on the continent, and contribute toward a better trained clergy in England.[35] Roger Bacon, writing about 1272, testified that "never was there such an appearance of learning, nor such an exercise of study in so many faculties and so many regions as during the past forty years. For everywhere teachers, especially in theology, are scattered about in every city, town and borough, particularly by the two student orders."[36] "Never before were there so many students and so many teachers. Now they lecture in every district, in every city and good town; and they preach everywhere."[37] This was in contrast with the fact that for the past forty years the seculars had been dependent on the friars for their education, even using their notes for lectures, disputations and sermons.[38] Bacon's complaints of the ignorance of the rural clergy, who understood little or nothing of the office they read,[39] and his account of how even bishops borrowed the sermon notes of young friars,[40] are apt to give an exaggerated notion of the conditions prevailing; but other writers of the time confirm his testimony as to the influence

32. Eccleston, pp. 60 *et seq.;* Felder, *op. cit.,* pp. 308-12.

33. Felder, *op. cit.,* pp. 312-13.

34. Little's note to Eccleston, p. 63.

35. See note 30, this chap., p. 131. On the friars as lectors in theology at cathedral schools, etc., see A. G. Little, "The Franciscan School at Oxford," *Archivum Franciscanum historicum,* XIX, 821.

36. Brewer, ed., *Compendium studii philosophiae,* R. S., p. 398.

37. *Ibid.,* p. 432.

38. *Ibid.,* 428-9.

39. *Ibid.,* p. 413.

40. *Ibid., Opus Tertium,* p. 309.

exercised by the friars on clerical education.[41] The ultimate benefits to society accruing thus directly and indirectly from the mendicants' pursuit of learning can hardly be overestimated.

Another great contribution which the friars made to medieval society was their promotion of international thought and activity, thus binding the nations together in greater unity and mutual understanding. The constant going and coming of these citizens of the world between all parts of Europe and Asia — as missionaries, delegates attending chapters and making visitations, students and lectors, papal, royal and municipal emissaries — encouraged an interchange of ideas and experiences and an international understanding which are hardly possible even in our own day, for all its means of rapid communication and transport; for today we have not a common language to take the place of Latin, nor have we the common bond of one religious faith. For evidence of this friendly intercommunication promoted by the friars we need only turn to their sermon *exempla,* chronicles, records of general chapters, and the numerous grants of permission to enter and leave the country printed in the Calendar of Patent Rolls.[42] Mr. Howlett calls attention to the central control of the Franciscan organization from Rome, and to other factors which "must have strengthened powerfully the sense of unity at the expense of that of nationality." But he emphasizes the claim that these things tended to upset the peace and good order of dioceses in England, and comes to the conclusion (it is not quite clear how) that the friars eventually lost England to the Church by refusing to be more national.[43] According to Mr. Howlett, the later Observants especially became "the chosen soldiers of the Pope," in a very

---

41. Felder, *op. cit.,* pp. 330-31; see St. Bonaventure on the prevalence of clerical ignorance, *Opera omnia,* VIII, 358, 378-9.

42. See, e.g., chaps. II *and* IV; *Lanercost Chronicle,* pp. 121, 129-30, 131, 135, 147-50; Eccleston and *Chronica Jordani, passim;* Friar Salimbene's gossipy account of his travels, *Mon. Germ. hist.,* XXXII; *Liber exemplorum,* B. S. F. S., vol. I, pp. ix, 44, 136, 192.

43. *Mon. Fran.,* II, xviii-xix, xliii-xliv.

real sense "the garrisons of a foreign belligerent power."[44] Their opposition to Henry VIII's divorce and his claims to be the head of the Church in England was in keeping with the character displayed by the friars over three centuries. "Historically fitting in every way, therefore, it seems [to Mr. Howlett] that the torch which lighted the final conflagration should have been actually applied by the hand of a follower of St. Francis."[45]

It does not fall within the scope of this essay to discuss the activities of fifteenth- and sixteenth-century Franciscans; but obviously, if the later friars were acting true to form in defending the papal supremacy, they can hardly be charged with responsibility for the rejection of this supremacy and the consequent withdrawal of England from Christian unity. Certainly, during the thirteenth and fourteenth centuries, when they could be more truly spoken of as "the chosen soldiers of the Pope," their influence was for unity and peace, however much they may have antagonized individuals and groups by their reform activities and their collecting of papal taxes.

These collecting activities were carried on mostly in connection with the crusades, and Matthew Paris repeatedly states that the friars did the collecting reluctantly.[46] The truth of this is borne out by a papal bull of 1253 exempting the Franciscans from the duty of preaching for money against their will.[47] But in spite of the fact that Paris claims that abuses in connection with crusade money led to a cooling off of the devotion of the people,[48] there seems to be no indication that the friars suffered in their popularity on that account. On the contrary, in so far as they promoted a movement which captivated the hearts and imaginations of all,

44. *Ibid.*, pp. xlii, xliii.
45. *Ibid.*, p. xliv.
46. *Chron. maj.*, V, 195, 260.
47. *Bullarium Fran.*, I, 670, the bull *Vestra semper,* Aug. 1, 1253. The friars are freed from this burden because it is recognized that by their life of poverty and freedom from financial cares "ad vestram, et proximorum salutem praedicationis officium liberius exercetis"; and they need not obey any order to the contrary "nisi litterae ipsae de hac indulgentia plenam fecerint mentionem."
48. *Chron. maj.*, III, 287; V, 73.

their crusade preaching must have enhanced their prestige. The solemnity with which the preaching was carried out and the general atmosphere created must have tended to the same result.

Here is Matthew Paris' description of the preaching of the crusade ordered by Pope Gregory IX in 1234: The preaching was done by the prelates, "but especially by the Friars Preachers and Minor, to whom was given the power of signing with the cross, and then, on the payment of money, of absolving from the vow; and a numberless multitude took the cross. But suddenly the Preachers and Minors, who have chosen voluntary poverty and humility, were raised to such nobility, not to say arrogance, that they had themselves received in the villages and towns by a solemn procession with banners, lighted candles and an array of people clad in festive garments. And they were allowed to give their hearers many days' grace, and those whom they signed with the cross today, they absolved from the vow of journey for a money payment on the morrow."[49]

The lukewarmness which this mercenary aspect of the crusades is supposed to have caused among the people must have been more than counteracted by such incidents as that which took place about this time in the village of Clare. A Franciscan, Master Roger of Lewes, was preaching the crusade when he was attracted by the groans and sighs of a certain woman in the audience. Taking pity on her, the preacher asked why she had ever come when she was so ill. She told him she feared excommunication if she did not attend. Not realizing her condition, the friar bade her go home. Then, learning that she had been deprived of the use of her limbs for three years past, and had spent her last farthing to hire a neighbor to carry her to church, the preacher turned to her and asked her: "Do you believe that God is powerful?" She answered in the words of the centurion: "I believe, Lord." "May

---

49. *Ibid.,* III, 287.

God in Whom you believe, cure you," prayed the friar; and the cripple was cured and walked home rejoicing.[50]

Paris later gives us another picture of crusade preaching, and expressly states that the ceremony attaching to it was designed to increase the devotion of the people. It was in 1249. "In these same times," runs the chronicle, "the Friars Preachers and Minor, at the command of the Lord Pope whom they obediently heeded, devoted themselves most earnestly and diligently to preaching; and in order to increase the devotion of the faithful, they approached with great solemnity the places for which their sermons had been previously announced. The priests and clerics met them in white vestments, with crosses and banners, accompanied by a large concourse of the faithful, as is the custom on Rogation Days. Preaching, therefore, the business of the cross, they signed people of whatever age, sex, rank or state of health — yea even the valetudinarians, the sick and those decrepit with age; and the next day, for whatever price they could get, they removed the cross from those they had signed and absolved all who wished from the vow of the journey."[51] And then Paris goes on to rail against the abuses in the use of the money thus collected and the scandal it gave the people.

His condemnation was probably not altogether unjustified; but there is no sufficient reason to believe that the friars were responsible for abuses in the use of the money. As to the collecting of it, be it remembered that the crusades were a popular undertaking, the common venture of a united Christendom. All were expected to take the cross in order to contribute each in his own way to the rescue of the Holy Places so dear to the hearts of all. Naturally, not all could make the journey to Palestine to fight the infidel; but large funds were needed to equip and transport an army, and to this all could contribute. Rich indulgences were attached to the journey to Palestine, and those unable to go might

---

50. Paris, *Chron. maj.*, III, 312-13.

51. *Chron. maj.*, V, 73.

gain similar indulgences by contributing to the crusade in some other way. In a milder mood Paris states that the friars "courteously received" whatever was offered them in order to give all a chance of helping along the cause.[52]

What especially opened the way to abuses was the extended notion sometimes attached to a crusade, for example, when Pope Innocent IV granted church tithes to Henry III for his Sicilian campaign.[53] There was a strong suspicion before this time, according to Paris, that the king was merely using the idea of a crusade as a pretext in order to raise money,[54] and that "like a baby" he ran to the Pope to prevent the crusading army from sailing.[55] When Henry finally did call together the nobles who had taken the cross and himself swore to go to the Holy Land, his motives were still suspected, and there was so strong a feeling among the bishops against the extortionate demands made on their churches that few were willing to coöperate.[56] This was between 1250 and 1252, about the time that Grosseteste and Adam Marsh were most active planning a reform of Church and State in England. And Bishop Grosseteste, for all his approval of crusades,[57] led the opposition against Henry's demands unless he promised to observe the Magna Carta and insure the liberties of the Church.[58] The bishops yielded to the king in 1253, but Grosseteste was dead when Henry's vow was commuted in 1254 to an expedition for the conquest of Sicily.[59] The bishop would almost certainly have disapproved of this new venture; and in general it might be said that the Franciscan attitude was that of Grosseteste. Henry requested the Franciscans to preach the cru-

---

52. *Hist. Anglorum,* III, 51-2, 308.
53. J. Lingard, *A History of England* (P. O'Shea, New York), III, 113.
54. *Chron. maj.,* V, 102-3.
55. *Ibid.,* p. 135.
56. *Ibid.,* pp. 279-81.
57. He collected money for the crusade in 1250. *Cal. Papal Letters,* I, 263.
58. Paris, *Chron. maj.,* V, 324-7, 335.
59. Treharne, *The Baronial Plan of Reform,* p. 60; Stevenson, *Robert Grosseteste,* pp. 302-5.

sade in 1254 and 1255, but with what results we do not know.[60] Adam Marsh urged William of Nottingham, the minister provincial, to accede to the king's request for crusade preachers, but it is not quite clear whether this was in 1251 or 1254.[61]

That the Franciscans in general approved of the crusades to Palestine there is no room for doubt; but like St. Francis, who left the crusaders' camp at Damietta in order to conquer the infidels by preaching,[62] they had no notion that armies were the ultimate solution of the Holy Land problem. Adam Marsh expressed the Franciscan attitude in these words: "Though the Catholic princes should be roused up to warlike action against the perfidious, ecclesiastical prelates must nevertheless never give up the work of preaching to the infidel."[63] Roger Bacon has little sympathy for the whole plan of using force against infidel peoples, because they "are not thus converted, but are killed and sent to hell."[64] He admits that the Holy Land should be in the hands of Christians and that this should be insured if necessary even by war;[65] but for the rest, war only embitters the infidels and makes their conversion practically impossible. Learn their language and preach to them — that is the thing to be done.[66]

This principle was followed by the English Franciscans to a very marked degree. True, they continued to preach the crusades until the end of the thirteenth century, negotiated crusade business and accompanied the crusaders. About the middle of the century the saintly Friar Robert of Thornham accompanied crusaders to Palestine,[67] as did Friar William of Heddele in 1270.[68]

---

60. *Cal. Pat., 1247-1258,* pp. 377, 440.
61. *Mon. Fran.,* I, 309. William was about to leave the country, probably on his way to the general chapter of Genoa in 1251, or to that of Metz in 1254.
62. *Chronica Jordani,* nos. 10 *et seq.*
63. *Mon. Fran.,* I, 416.
64. *Opus majus,* edn. Bridges, III, 121; see also *Opus Tert.,* R. S., p. 88.
65. *Ibid.,* III, 122.
66. *Ibid.,* III, 121-2. Bacon makes the observation that the Prussians and other peoples bordering on Germany would have been converted long since had it not been for the violence of the Teutonic Knights.
67. Eccleston, pp. 110-11; *Mon. Fran.,* I, 551.
68. See chap. IV, p. 80.

Another English friar, one-time guardian of Oxford, was hacked to death while carrying the cross against the Saracens who attacked Tripoli in 1289.[69] In 1276 Archbishop Giffard enlisted the friars to preach the crusade in his diocese and commanded the people and clergy to assemble to hear them "wherever and as often as they [the friars] think expedient."[70] In 1291 Archbishop Romanus had the Franciscans supply crusade preachers in some sixteen places throughout his jurisdiction.[71] About the same time Pope Nicholas IV, himself a Franciscan, called upon the Franciscans and Dominicans in both England and Ireland to promote the crusade,[72] while Edward I engaged a friar of each order to negotiate a delay of the crusade till the summer of 1293.[73] Though Edward I never gave up the idea of leading an army to Palestine, the age of the crusades was really past.

Not so the English Franciscan interest in the Holy Land and the Near East; and this interest must have been a powerful factor all along in keeping alive the enthusiasm of the people. The stories of their heroic and saintly *confrères* who gave their lives for the conversion of the pagans and the rescue of the Holy Places must have offered unsurpassed sermon material for the friars who preached the crusades. Miracles are said to have occurred at the death of Adam of Oxford, one of the first of the English Franciscans to give his life for the spread of Christianity among the Saracens.[74] The same was the case with Robert of Thornham.[75] Haymo of Faversham and Ralph of Rheims must have had interesting things to relate of their mission to Patriarch Germanus of

---

69. *Lanercost Chronicle,* p. 128.
70. *Historical Papers and Letters from the Northern Registers,* p. 46.
71. *Ibid.,* p. 95.
72. *Cal. Papal Letters,* I, 553.
73. *Ibid.,* p. 551. See notes to *Lanercost Chronicle,* pp. 487-89, on the two Franciscans sent by the king of Armenia to Edward I to explain conditions in the Holy Land.
74. Eccleston, pp. 21, 23. Adam was a friend of Bishop Grosseteste, who wrote a letter of consolation to Blessed Agnellus and his brethren at Oxford on Adam's departure for the missions. Golubovich dates this departure as 1231-2. (*Biblioteca bio-bibliografica etc.,* I, 295).
75. Eccleston, pp. 110-11.

Constantinople in 1233-1234.[76] And these accounts not only edified the people and quickened their Christian faith and sense of unity, but widened the horizons of knowledge. Both Bartholomew the Englishman and Roger Bacon wrote of the Holy Land and adjacent parts[77] and their knowledge was probably supplied by missionaries. Bacon certainly used William Rubruk's account of his journey to the court of the Great Khan in central Mongolia, and spoke with the author himself.[78]

As early as 1237 Pope Gregory IX, realizing that the friars' efforts to convert the pagans were just as meritorious as fighting the perfidious Saracens, had granted to the Franciscans and Dominicans who undertook foreign missionary work the same indulgences which were granted to the crusaders.[79] And the friars' peaceful crusade endured long after the warlike crusades had ended. In 1313 King Edward II granted letters engrossed and sealed with the great seal to "some Friars Minor to go to preach the faith in the Holy Land."[80] Friar William Walden of England was martyred by the Saracens at Salamascus in Persia in 1342.[81] Friar John the Englishman was martyred in Illyria in 1343.[82] And there must have been many another uncommemorated English

---

76. *Archivum Franciscanum historicum,* XII, 418 *et seq.* The mission was sent by Pope Gregory IX to try to effect peace and unity with the Eastern Church. Ralph of Rheims was of English descent.

77. *De proprietatibus rerum,* Lib. XV, Cap. lxxvi, cxiiii, etc.; *Opus majus,* edn. of Bridges, I, 335-50.

78. *Opus majus,* I, 268, 305.

79. *Bullarium Franciscanum,* I, 233.

80. *Cal. Chancery Warrants, 1244-1326,* p. 390.

81. *Mon. Fran.,* I, 528. Golubovich, *op. cit.,* IV, 235 and VI, 76, appears to be confused on the date.

82. *Analecta Franciscana,* Quaracchi, III, 529. He is probably the same as John Clotsdale, an English Franciscan who was honored as a saint in parts beyond the sea. The date of their death is the same (Kingsford, *Grey Friars of London,* p. 182).

For other activities of English Franciscans in the Holy Land, etc., see Golubovich, *op. cit.,* I, 100, 231, 266-9, 276, 280-81; II, 295, 346-9, 369, 404-11; III, 155-6, 394; IV, 235, 395; VI, 76.

For crusade preaching by Franciscans in other lands, see *Archivum Franciscanum historicum,* IX, 99-117; Anscar Zawart, *The History of Franciscan Preaching and Preachers: 1209-1927* (*Franciscan Studies,* VII, St. Anthony Guild Press, Paterson, N. J., 1928), pp. 248-250 and references.

Franciscan who labored for the spread of the faith in foreign parts and thus kept alive also the faith at home and the sense of man's brotherhood with all men.

Another important service which the Franciscans rendered to society was that of peacemaking. The spirit of their organization, their learning, their popularity and their wandering life all combined to equip them for this task. Before his conversion, St. Francis had taken part in the petty wars which tore his native land. His call to a new life came to him in the midst of a warlike expedition. But thereafter he was a man of peace.[83] "The Lord give you peace" became his greeting,[84] and he set about trying to extinguish the quarrels which disturbed his countrymen.[85] Francis and his followers were aware that there could be no real revival of Christian living as long as hatreds rankled in men's hearts and mutual love, the prime test of a Christian was lacking. Men must be brought together in peace and harmony and the worst evils in society will disappear. Having stripped themselves of property and worldly ambition, the Friars Minor could preach peace by word and example and their motives could not be questioned.

The English brethren carried on the work of peacemaking in the best Franciscan tradition. The saintly Friar Agnellus, who knew St. Francis, is the first among them of whom we have record to act as peacemaker in an important case. Henry III's rather arbitrary rule under foreign advisers was a source of perpetual unrest. In 1233 Richard Marshal, Earl of Pembroke, complained of Henry's unfairness and rebelled against his authority. War was imminent, but Agnellus spared no efforts to prevent bloodshed. Roger Wendover gives a detailed account of the friar's negotiations with Richard at Margam Abbey in South Wales.[86] He tells us that Agnellus was a close friend and counselor of the king,

83. Father Cuthbert, *Life of St. Francis,* pp. 17-19.
84. *Ibid.,* p. 100.
85. *Ibid.,* pp. 101, 332, 357.
86. *Chronicle,* R. S., III, 64 *et seq.*

probably one of those friars whom, according to Matthew Paris,[87] Henry was accustomed to heed and who had pleaded with him to show more love for his subjects. It is evident from the conversations that Agnellus was thoroughly acquainted with Henry and his court; and one is struck by the tone of authority with which the friar reasoned with the embittered earl to submit to the king, "because it was his duty, it was to his advantage and it was safe" to do so. But Richard's respect for Agnellus and the Church was not sufficient to overcome his distrust of Henry and his advisers, and the friar pleaded in vain. Richard's distrust was natural enough after so many broken promises from the king, and it was rather justified by the events which followed. The next year the earl was basely betrayed to death by a royal agent, and buried, according to one account, by his own request in the Franciscan church at Kilkenny.[88]

The meeting between Agnellus and the Earl Marshal took place "on the Thursday before Christmas," which in 1233 fell on a Sunday; and one can well suppose that the approach of this feast whetted the efforts of the devoted follower of the saint who "cherished the Nativity of the Child Jesus with ineffable eagerness above other feasts."[89] It is not impossible that Agnellus had been with St. Francis at Greccio just ten years before, when the saint inaugurated that novel and impressive dramatization of Christmas which gave rise to our Christmas crib.[90] Agnellus surely spent himself to establish that peace and brotherly love which Christmas is meant to bring. Shortly after his unsuccessful mission, Agnellus "fell sick at Oxford of dysentery from the cold, as it was said, and the labor which he bore in order to establish peace between the Lord King of England and his Marshal on the border

87. *Chron. maj.*, III, 251.

88. Thus Wendover's account, *Chronicle*, III, 81-7. Others, rather more probably, say the earl was buried in the Dominican church. See *Materials for the History of the Franciscan Province of Ireland*, B. S. F. S., vol. IX, p. 3 and references.

89. Celano, II, 199; edn. of E. d'Alencon, p. 318.

90. Father Cuthbert, *Life of St. Francis*, pp. 329 *et seq.*

of Wales, and in traveling about through England."[91] From this sickness he never recovered.[92]

In the rôle of peacemaker, Adam Marsh was a worthy disciple of Francis and Agnellus. He not only used every means to compose the difficulties between Henry III and Simon de Montfort,[93] but was constantly writing letters in the interest of peace and harmony. He tried to reconcile the Earl of Leicester and the Earl of Toulouse,[94] the Abbot of Dorchester and the Abbess of Godstow,[95] the Bishop and the Convent of Winchester;[96] and there were many others, most notably Queen Eleanor and the Earl of Cornwall.[97] He was furthermore urged by Archbishop Boniface to attend an assembly of prelates in order to help to appease dissensions in the kingdom;[98] was delegated by the Pope to arbitrate in the differences between the king and the Bishop of St. David's, and between this same bishop and the Abbot of Gloucester;[99] and was sent abroad by the king to "treat of peace between Louis, King of France, and the king and his heirs, touching all controversies and questions."[100]

Friar John Pecham continued the tradition. Pecham's, to be sure, was not a peace-at-any-price attitude. He loved justice and the poor too much for that. Peace, however desirable, must give way to justice and morality; or rather, the latter must form the basis of peace. There are principles worth fighting for. We shall not dwell on the archbishop's efforts to reconcile the quarreling factions among the Canterbury monks,[101] to calm the dissensions in Merton College, Oxford,[102] to arbitrate between his own offi-

91. Eccleston, pp. 94-5.
92. *Ibid.*, p. 95. He died probably in 1236 (*ibid.*, p. 95, note).
93. See chap. III, pp. 57-58.
94. *Mon. Fran.*, I, 381.
95. *Ibid.*, p. 209.
96. *Ibid.*, p. 85.
97. *Ibid.*, p. 291.
98. *Ibid.*, pp. 343-4.
99. *Ibid.*, p. 342.
100. *Cal. Pat., 1247-1258*, p. 594.
101. *Register*, Letter 301, pp. 389-90; see also pp. 339-48; 388 *et seq.*
102. *Ibid.*, Letter 106, pp. 123-4.

cial and the Prior of Lewes,[103] to reconcile Edmund, Earl of Cornwall, and his wife;[104] or on the many letters he wrote in the interests of justice, charity and a better understanding between various individuals and groups under his jurisdiction. His attempts in 1282 to promote a peaceful settlement between Edward I and Llewellyn, leader of the Welsh nationals, give a sufficient insight into his character.

Though he had already in April excommunicated the Welsh who were disturbing the peace,[105] Pecham was ready "for the honor of the Lord King and the good of the most foolish Welsh people to expose himself to labors, expenses and dangers for the public peace."[106] In October he sent Friar John of Wales ahead to open negotiations with the Welsh,[107] and a little later undertook to go in person with the hope of "turning them from their evil ways by wholesome counsel and bringing them back to Catholic unity."[108] King Edward resented the interference of Pecham, but the archbishop realized that if he withdrew there would be no one to take up the task; and therefore he was willing, if it so pleased God, to procure an honest and stable peace at the price of his life.[109] Llewellyn welcomed the archbishop's intervention and protested his readiness to second his prayers and efforts, though he complained of the cruelty and faithlessness of the English.[110] The Welsh then submitted a long list of grievances[111] which Pecham reported to Edward. In the meantime, while the grievances were being considered, the English army under Luke de Tany treacherously violated the truce and attacked the Welsh at Snowdon. When the English were defeated in the battle, Llewellyn proved less willing than ever to accept Edward's severe terms

103. *Ibid.*, Letter 464, pp. 593-4.
104. *Ibid.*, Letter 703, pp. 969-70.
105. *Ibid.*, Letter 254, pp. 324-5.
106. *Ibid.*, Letter 301, pp. 389-90.
107. *Ibid.*, Letter 327, pp. 421-2.
108. *Ibid.*, Letter 332, p. 426.
109. *Ibid.*, Letter 340, pp. 435-7.
110. *Ibid.*, Letter 341, pp. 437-40.
111. *Ibid.*, Letters 342-52, pp. 440-65.

of absolute submission for himself and the perpetual banishment of his brother David.[112] The negotiations had to be abandoned as hopeless, and Pecham returned home bitterly reproaching the Welsh and insulting their national pride.[113]

One might point to Pecham's somewhat patronizing and pro-English tone throughout the discussions, and especially his bitter denunciations of the Welsh after negotiations had failed, as indicating qualities ill-befitting a peacemaker. On the other hand, we must respect his firmness in refusing to countenance rebellion against what he considered lawful authority. As a prince of the Church he was unable to approve of insubordination and of many of the local Welsh customs, which he recognized as contrary to Christianity, but in non-essential points he was ready to make concessions. The treachery of the English and the unyielding attitude of Edward were chiefly responsible for the ultimate failure of his arbitration. At least Pecham's heart was right. His thankless task cost him not only grave inconveniences but considerable monetary losses as well.[114] After the rebellion had been put down, Pecham again returned to Wales "to occupy himself with that torn and lacerated people."[115] He insisted that Edward make restitution for the destruction of church property and other crimes committed by the English army against the Welsh.[116]

Nor were John Pecham and John of Wales the only Franciscans concerned with bringing about peaceful relations between the English and the Welsh. Before there was a question of open conflict, Friar William de Merton, warden of the Friars Minor of Llanfaes, was employed by Llewellyn as a peace messenger to King Edward.[117] And it appears that some sort of settlement had

112. *Ibid.,* pp. 465-73. On the treacherous attack at Snowdon, see *Annales mon.,* IV, 289, and J. E. Morris, *The Welsh Wars of Edward the First* (Oxford, 1901), pp. 179-80.

113. *Register,* Letter 360, pp. 473-7.

114. *Ibid.,* Letter 376, pp. 494-5.

115. *Ibid.,* Letter 519; also 509, 537, 552, 558, etc.

116. *Ibid.,* Letter 558, pp. 731-5.

117. J. Goronwy Edwards, ed., *Calendar of Ancient Correspondence Concerning Wales* (Oxford, 1935), pp. 62, 89-90, 96, 99, 100, etc.

been reached through the friar's efforts when misunderstanding or some new complications gave rise to further troubles.[118] Friar William himself wrote to Edward in behalf of Llewellyn "from the zeal which he has for the continuance of peace between them," and with great respect and deference informed the king that Llewellyn had just cause for complaint.[119] The Franciscan influence on Llewellyn is further suggested by the manner in which he dates one of his letters, "in crastino B. Francisci."[120] Throughout the correspondence between the two rulers, however, there are references to obstructions in the way of peaceful settlement. It would be interesting to know who was really responsible for these.

Superficially viewed, these Franciscan peace efforts did little good. Failure appears to have stalked in the wake of all of them. So it also did with another and earlier effort recorded by Matthew Paris. In 1241 the English bishops and other ecclesiastics assembled in council decided to try to end the scandalous war between the emperor and the Pope. Accordingly they would send messengers to Frederick II begging him to cease hostilities. But when it came to selecting the messengers, no one could be found who was willing to undertake the dangerous journey. Finally, after all the prelates had made excuses, it was decided to send the Friars Preachers and Minor, because a "penniless traveler can sing in the face of a robber," and because the friars were "vagrants who know how to make their way swiftly through all the provinces."[121] But Frederick's anger against Rome was too deep-seated to be appeased, and he had a grievance against the English inasmuch as they were supplying the Pope with money. Besides, this was one instance where the friars were hardly acceptable mes-

---

118. *Ibid.,* Llewellyn's letter of July 6 (1280).

119. *Ibid.,* pp. 99, 100.

120. *Ibid.,* pp. 87-88. In 1261 two Welsh Franciscans and two Dominicans acted as arbitrators between Prince Llewellyn and Richard, Bishop of Bangor; see R. C. Easterling, "The Friars in Wales," *Archaeologia Cambrensis,* XIV, 6th Series (London, 1914), 333.

121. *Chron. maj.,* IV, 173: "Tandem, quia 'Cantabit vacuus coram latrone viator' (Juvenal, X, 22) Praedicatores et Minores, quia vagi sunt et norunt omnes provincias peragrare expediti, ad hoc elegerunt."

sengers of peace. Frederick hated them for the part they took against him in Italy;[122] and later he and his son Conrad were to place guards all about to intercept the friars who traveled to and from the papal court in disguise bearing messages and money. When captured they were tortured and hanged.[123]

The instances, though, when the Franciscans were not acceptable peacemakers could not have been many; and if they failed to all outward appearances in most of their efforts, the fault was not lack of zeal and good-will. In appraising the results, we must not forget that the very efforts put forth and the fact that they were given a respectful hearing at all was something of a victory for the peaceful spirit the friars represented. Who will say that nothing was accomplished even when they seemed to fail? To have set an example and preached the doctrine of Christian brotherhood and peace must have tempered the cruelties of the conflict even when they were not prevented. The efforts of Adam Marsh, William of Gainsborough and other Franciscans to bring about a settlement between England and France were surely not altogether in vain. Treaties and truces were effected, and the principle of arbitration received greater recognition.[124] The same may be said of the negotiations in which the friars took part after the battle of Lewes, and of the other diplomatic missions in which they were engaged.[125] The fact that they were universally recognized as arbiters, even when they served some particular interest or ruler, argues for the peaceful influence of the friars.

In private disputes between individuals and families their peaceful influence was probably more effective, for the masses were more amenable to their word and example and there was less suspicion of partisanship in petty quarrels. We do not know

---

122. *Ibid.,* III, 636.

123. *Ibid.,* III, 636; IV, 256, 278, 551.

124. See this chap., p. 143; chap. IV, pp. 88 *et seq.; Foedera,* I, 861, 877, 884.

125. See chap. III, pp. 61 etc.; chap. IV, *passim.*

how many of Adam Marsh's or John Pecham's pleas for peace and reconciliation were attended with success. Neither do we know how many unrecorded cases of a similar nature were settled by their *confrères.* The case of the Gascony friars who came to Henry III asking permission for intermarriage between certain families "for the perpetual strengthening of the peace,"[126] and that of Friar Roger of Canterbury's putting his seal upon a peaceful settlement between two merchants,[127] must have had parallels elsewhere.[128] But only exceptionally would the more or less routine labors of the friars for sweet harmony and good-will among the little ones of Christ's flock find their way into written records.

And it is on this note that the writer wishes to conclude, a note of tribute to those unsung, anonymous friars who went about doing good among their fellow-men in the spirit of the Man of Galilee Whom they followed with such ardor. Their devotion to pure evangelical Christianity is one of the phenomena of history. All things to all men they truly were, and to a remarkable extent they did win all men for Christ. If the ideal for which they stood suffered in its contact with the world, the world nevertheless profited from it beyond calculation. Art, literature, social relations, religion, man in all his works, have felt its influence. The lives of those professing devotion to this ideal have not always been beyond reproach, but the ideal itself has never ceased to attract; and like Christianity itself, of which it is but an interpretation, it continues to be revived and adapted to new generations of men and new problems of human life.

126. *Cal. Pat., 1247-1258,* p. 608.
127. *Ibid.,* pp. 591-2.
128. See chap. IV, p. 83-4; *Cal. Close, 1272-1279* p. 232; *Cal. Pat., 1247-1258,* p. 522; *Cal. Papal Letters,* I, 600, 605, 607; II, 183, etc.

BIBLIOGRAPHY

An asterisk (*) indicates one of the more generally useful works.

General Works

1. *Analecta Franciscana,* 5 vols. Quaracchi, 1885-1912.
2. *Archivum Franciscanum historicum,* Vols. IX, XII, XIX. Quaracchi, 1907—.
3. *Bliss, W. H., ed., *Calendar of Papal Letters,* Vols. I-III. London, 1893-97.
4. *Dictionary of National Biography.* London, 1885; Oxford, 1917.
5. Eubel, ed., *Bullarium Franciscanum,* Vol. V. Rome, 1898.
6. G. E. C., *Complete Peerage,* 8 vols. London, 1887-98.
7. Hardy, ed., Syllabus of Rymer's *Foedera,* Vol. I. London, 1869.
8. Le Neve, *Fasti ecclesiae Anglicanae,* edited by Hardy. Oxford, 1854.
9. Migne, ed., *Bibliotheca patrum Latina,* Vol. 190. Paris, 1884.
10. Potthast, A., *Regesta Pontificum Romanorum,* 2 vols. Berlin, 1874-5.
11. Rymer, *Foedera,* Vols. I-III. London, 1816-30.
12. *Sbaralea, ed., *Bullarium Franciscanum,* Vols. I-IV and Supplement. Rome, 1759-80.
13. Sbaralea, H., *Supplementum et castigatio ad scriptores Trium Ordinum S. Francisci.* Rome, 1806.
14. Wadding, *Annales Minorum,* Vols. I-VIII. Quaracchi, 1931—.

Printed Records

A. Ecclesiastical

1. Episcopal Registers

Bath and Wells:

Calendar of the Register of John de Drokensford. Somerset Rec. Soc., 1887.

Exeter Registers, edited by Hingeston-Randolph. Vols. I-IV, 1889-99.

Hereford:

Thomas de Cantilupe. Canterbury and York Soc., Vol. II, 1906.

Richard de Swinfield. Canterbury and York Soc., Vol. VI, 1909.

Thomas Charlton. Canterbury and York Soc., Vol. IX, 1912.
Historical Papers and Letters from the Northern Registers. Rolls Series.
Registrum epistolarum Fratris J. Peckham. Rolls Series.
Roberti Grosseteste epistolae. Rolls Series.
Winchester:
John de Pontissara. Canterbury and York Soc., Vols. XIX and XXIX, 1915 and 1924.
John de Sandale and Rigaud de Asserio. Hampshire Rec. Soc., 1893.
York:
Walter Giffard. Surtees Soc., Vol. 109, 1904.
William Wickwane. Surtees Soc., Vol. 114, 1907.
John le Romeyn. Surtees Soc., Vols. 123 and 128, 1913 and 1916.
Thomas Corbridge. Surtees Soc., Vol. 138, 1925.

2. Chronicles

Annales monastici, 4 vols. and index. Rolls Series.
Celano, Thomas de, *S. Francisci Assisiensis vita et miracula,* edited by P. Edouard d'Alencon. Rome, 1906.
Chronica de Mailros. Edinburgh, 1835; English translation by Jos. Stevenson in *Church Historians of England,* Vol. IV, London, 1856.
Chronica maiorum et vicecomitum Londoniarum (and *Liber de Antiquis Legibus*). Camden Soc., Vol. 34, 1846.
Chronicles of the Reigns of Edward I and Edward II, 2 vols. Rolls Series.
*Eccleston, Thomas de, *De adventu Fratrum Minorum in Angliam,* edited by A. G. Little, Paris, 1909; English translation by Father Cuthbert, London, 1909.
Flores historiarum, Vols. II and III. Rolls Series.
Froissart, *Chronicles,* Vol. I. Edited by S. Luce, Paris, 1869.
Gervase of Canterbury and Continuator, *Historical Works,* Vol. II. Rolls Series.
Hemingburgh, Walter de, *Chronicon,* 2 vols. Edited by H. C. Hamilton, London, 1848-9.
Jordanus, Frater, *Chronica Jordani,* edited by H. Boehmer. Paris, 1908.
Knighton, Henry, *Chronicon,* 2 vols. Rolls Series.
**Lanercost Chronicle,* edited by Jos. Stevenson. Edinburgh, 1839; part in English by Sir Herbert Maxwell, Glasgow, 1913.
Memorials of St. Edmund's Abbey, Vols. II and III. Rolls Series.
*Paris, Matthew, *Chronica majora,* Vols. III-V. Rolls Series.
————————*Historia Anglorum,* Vols. II and III. Rolls Series.
Peterburgh Chronicle, edited by Jos. Sparke in *Historiae Anglicanae scriptores varii.* London, 1723.
Rishanger, *Chronica et annales.* Rolls Series.
Robert of Gloucester, *Metrical Chronicle.* Rolls Series.

Salimbene, *Cronica Fratris Salimbene de Adam,* in *Monumenta Germaniae historica,* Vol. XXXII. Hannover, 1905.
Trivet, Fr. Nicholas, *Annales,* edited by T. Hog. London, 1845.
Wendover, Roger de, *Chronicle,* Vol. III. Rolls Series.
Walsingham, Thomas de, *Gesta abbatum,* 3 vols. Rolls Series.
———————*Historia Anglicana,* 2 vols. Rolls Series.
———————*Ypodigma Neustriae.* Rolls Series.

3. Other Works

Bacon, Roger, *Opera adhuc inedita* (*Opus tertium, Opus minus, Compendium studii philosophiae*). Rolls Series.
———————*Opus Majus,* edited by J. H. Bridges, 3 vols. Oxford, 1897-1900.
———————*Compendium studii theologiae,* edited by H. Rashdall. British Society of Franciscan Studies, Vol. III, Aberdeen, 1911.
———————*Greek Grammar of . . . Hebrew Grammar,* edited by Nolan and Hirsch. Cambridge, 1902.
Bartholomew the Englishman, *De proprietatibus rerum.* Nuremburg, 1519.
Bonaventure, St., *Opera omnia,* Vol. VIII. Quaracchi, 1898.
*Bozon, *Les contes moralises de Nicole Bozon,* edited by Lucy Toulmin Smith and M. Paul Meyer. Paris, 1889; English translation by J. R., *The Metaphors of Brother Bozon.* London, 1913.
Brown, Carleton, ed., *English Lyrics of the Thirteenth Century.* Oxford, 1932.
———————*Religious Lyrics of the Fourteenth Century.* Oxford, 1924.
Fasciculi zizaniorum. Rolls Series.
Halliwell, J. O., ed., *Miracles of Simon de Montfort.* Camden Soc., Vol. XV, 2, London, 1840.
*Little, A. G., ed., *Liber exemplorum.* British Society of Franciscan Studies, Aberdeen, 1908.
Litterae Cantuarienses, Vols. I and II. Rolls Series.
**Monumenta Franciscana,* 2 vols. Rolls Series.
Pecock, Reginald, *The Repressor,* Rolls Series.
Robinson, Paschal, ed., *The Writings of St. Francis of Assisi.* Philadelphia, 1906.
Sabatier, Paul, ed., *Speculum perfectionis.* Paris, 1898.
Wales, John of, *Summa collationum.* Paris, 1516.
Wilkins, David, *Concilia,* Vols. I-III. London, 1737.

B. Civil

1. Bart, Sir T. P., ed., *Rotulus Walliae,* Part I. Cheltenham, 1865.
2. *Calendar of Chancery Warrants, 1244-1326.* Stationery Office, London.

3. **Calendar of Close Rolls, 1272-1354* (*Close Rolls, 1227-1264*). Stationery Office, London.
4. **Calendar of Patent Rolls, 1232-1350* (*Patent Rolls, 1225-1232*). Stationery Office, London.
5. Cole, H., ed., *Documents Illustrative of English History in the Thirteenth and Fourteenth Centuries.* London, 1884.
6. Edwards, J. Goronwy, ed., *Calendar of Ancient Correspondence concerning Wales.* Oxford, 1935.
7. Johnstone, Hilda, ed., *Letters of Edward, Prince of Wales, 1304-1305.* Cambridge, 1931.
8. Kingsford, C. L., ed., *The Song of Lewes.* Oxford, 1890.
9. Salter, H., ed., *The Oxford Deeds of Balliol College.* Oxford, 1913.
10. Stevenson, Jos., ed., *Documents Illustrative of the History of Scotland,* 2 vols. Edinburgh, 1870.
11. Wright, Thomas, ed., *The Political Songs of England.* Camden Soc., Vol. VI, London, 1839.
12. *Testamenta Eboracensia.* Surtees Soc., Vol. CVI, 1902.

Later Works

Allen, C. K., *Law in the Making.* Oxford, 1927.

Ashley, W. J., *The Bread of Our Forefathers.* Oxford, 1928.

*Bateson, Mary, *Mediaeval England.* London, 1903.

Bémont, Charles, *Simon de Montfort.* English translation by E. F. Jacob. Oxford, 1930.

Bourdillon, A. F. C., *The Order of Minoresses in England.* British Society of Franciscan Studies, Vol. XII, Manchester, 1926.

Bridges, J. H., *The Life and Work of Roger Bacon,* edited by Gordon Jones. London, 1914.

Bryce, Moir, *The Scottish Grey Friars,* 2 vols. Edinburgh, 1909.

Clay, R. M., *The Mediaeval Hospitals of England.* London, 1909.

Collectanea Franciscana, II. British Society of Franciscan Studies, Vol. X, Manchester, 1922.

Cuthbert, Father, O. S. F. C., *Life of St. Francis of Assisi.* London, 1912.

*Davies, W. C., ed., *Mediaeval England.* Oxford, 1924.

Deansley, Margaret, *The Lollard Bible and Other Mediaeval Biblical Versions.* Cambridge, 1920.

Essays in Mediaeval History Presented to Thomas Tout. Manchester, 1925.

Fletcher, W. G. D., *The Black Friars of Oxford.* Oxford, 1882.

Felder, Fr. Hilarin, *Geschichte der wissenschaftlichen Studien im Franziskanerorden bis um die Mitte des 13. Jahrhunderts.* Freiburg, 1904.

Fitzmaurice, E. B., and A. G. Little, *Materials for the History of the Franciscan Province of Ireland.* British Society of Franciscan Studies, Vol. IX, Manchester, 1920.

Franciscus a S. Clara (Christopher Davenport), *Manuale missionariorum regularium praecipue Anglorum S. Francisci.* Douai, 1661.
Graham, Rose, *English Ecclesiastical Studies.* London, 1929.
Golubovich, Fr. Girolamo, *Biblioteca bio-bibliografica della Terra Santa,* 6 vols. Quaracchi, 1906-30.
Goad, H. E., *Franciscan Italy.* London, 1926.
Grundmann, Herbert, *Religioese Bewegungen im Mittelalter* (*Historische Studien,* Heft 267). Berlin, 1935.
Historical Essays in Honour of James Tait. Manchester, 1933.
Hutton, Edward, *The Franciscans in England, 1224-1538.* London, 1926.
Joergensen, Johannes, *St. Francis of Assisi.* English translation by T. O'Conor Sloane, London, 1912.
Jacob, E. F., *Studies in the Period of Baronial Reform and Rebellion.* Oxford, 1925.
*Kingsford, C. L., *The Grey Friars of London.* British Society of Franciscan Studies, Vol. VI, Aberdeen, 1915.
Koch, Adolf, *Die fruehesten Niederlassungen der Minoriten im Rheingebiet,* Leipzig, 1881.
*Lenhart, J. M., *Science in the Franciscan Order.* FRANCISCAN STUDIES, I, St. Anthony Guild Press, Paterson, N. J.
*Little, A. G., *The Grey Friars in Oxford.* Oxford, 1892.
——————*Studies in English Franciscan History.* Manchester, 1917.
——————and F. Pelster, *Oxford Theology and Theologians.* Oxford, 1934.
——————and R. C. Easterling, *The Franciscans and Dominicans of Exeter.* Exeter, 1927.
*Lutz, E., *Roger Bacon's Contribution to Knowledge.* FRANCISCAN STUDIES, XVII, St. Anthony Guild Press, Paterson, N. J., 1936.
Morris, J. E., *The Welsh Wars of Edward the First.* Oxford, 1901.
Mueller, Karl, *Die Anfaenge des Minoritenordens und der Bussbruderschaften.* Freiburg, 1885.
Oman, Charles, *The Great Revolt of 1381.* Oxford, 1906.
Opuscules de critique historique, Vol. I. Paris, 1903.
Owst, G. R., *Preaching in Medieval England.* Cambridge, 1926.
Parkinson, Fr. Cuthbert, *Collectanea Anglo-Minoritica.* London, 1726.
Pauli, Reinhold, *Bilder aus Alt-England.* London, 1860.
——————*Simon de Montfort, Earl of Leicester.* English translation by E. M. Goodwin, London, 1876.
Pollock and Maitland, *The History of English Law.* Cambridge, 1895.
Prothero, G. W., *Simon de Montfort.* London, 1877.
Réville, André, *Le soulèvement des travailleurs d'Angleterre en 1381;* Historical Introduction by Ch. Petit-Dutaillis. Paris, 1898.
Sever, *The English Franciscans under Henry III.* Oxford, 1915.

Scholz, Richard, *Unbekannte kirchenpolitische Streitschriften aus der Zeit Ludwigs des Bayern,* 2 vols. Rome, 1911-1914.

Sharp, D. E., *Franciscan Philosophy at Oxford.* British Society of Franciscan Studies, Vol. XVI, Oxford, 1930.

Steele, Robert, *Medieval Lore.* London, 1893.

*Stevenson, F. S., *Robert Grosseteste.* London, 1899.

Tawney, R. H., *Religion and the Rise of Capitalism.* London, 1926.

Tout, T. F., *Chapters in Administrative History of Mediaeval England,* Vol. III. Manchester, 1920.

Transactions of the Royal Historical Society. 4th Series, X, New Series, VIII.

Treharne, R. F., *The Baronial Plan of Reform.* Manchester, 1932.

**The Victoria History of the Counties of England.* Doubleday, Page, etc., London.

*Wegemer, L., and V. Mayer, *St. Bonaventure, the Seraphic Doctor.* FRANCISCAN STUDIES, II, St. Anthony Guild Press, Paterson, N. J.

Wood-Legh, K. L., *Studies in Church Life in England under Edward III.* Cambridge, 1934.

*Zawart, Fr. Anscar, *The History of Franciscan Preaching and Preachers (1209-1927).* FRANCISCAN STUDIES, VII, St. Anthony Guild Press, Paterson, N. J., 1928.

PERIODICALS

The Antiquary, Vols. XXII-XXIII. London.

American Historical Review. July, 1919.

Archaeologia, Vols. LXXV and LXXIX. London.

Archaeologia Cambrensis, Vol. XIV, 6th Series. London.

The Archaeological Journal, Vol. LIX. London.

**The English Historical Review,* Vols. VII, XXXI, XXXIII, XXXIV, XL, XLIV, XLIX, etc. London.

The Dublin Review. April, 1925.

Journal of the Chester and North Wales Archaeological and Historical Society, New Series, Vol. XXIV.

Oxford Historical Society (Snappe's Formulary), Vol. LXXX. Oxford, 1924.

The Wiltshire Archaeological and Natural History Magazine, Vol. XLVII, No. CLXII. June, 1935.

APPENDIX I

Custodies and Friaries of the English Franciscans

From *Provinciale vetustissimum,* list of c. 1343, supplemented and annotated by A. G. Little in Eccleston's *De adventu* (Paris, 1909), pp. 149-54, with dates of foundation.

Custody of London

1. London, 1224
2. Salisbury, before 1230
3. Canterbury, 1224
4. Winchelsea, before 1253
5. Southampton, before 1235
6. Lewes, before 1231
7. Winchester, 1237
8. Chichester, before 1253

Custody of Oxford

1. Oxford, 1224
2. Reading, 1233
3. Bedford, before 1242
4. Stamford, before 1230
5. Nottingham, before 1230
6. Northampton, 1225
7. Leicester, before 1230
8. Grantham, before 1290

Custody of Bristol

1. Bristol, before 1230
2. Bridgewater, before 1245
3. Exeter, before 1240
4. Dorchester, before 1267
5. Bodmin, before 1280 (1239?)
6. Gloucester, before 1230
7. Hereford, before 1228
8. Carmarthen, before 1284
9. Cardiff, before 1304

Custody of Cambridge

1. Cambridge, before 1230 (?)
2. Norwich, 1226
3. Bury St. Edmund's, 1233 (Babwell, 1257)
4. King's Lynn, c. 1230
5. Yarmouth, before 1271
6. Ipswich, before 1236
7. Colchester, before 1237
8. Dunwich, before 1290

Custody of Worcester

1. Worcester, c. 1227
2. Coventry, before 1241
3. Lichfield, c. 1237
4. Stafford, before 1282
5. Preston, 1260 or before
6. Shrewsbury, 1245-6
7. Chester, c. 1238-40
8. Llanfaes, 1245
9. Bridgenorth, 1244

Custody of York

1. York, before 1236
2. Lincoln, 1230
3. Beverley, before 1267
4. Doncaster, before 1290
5. Boston, before 1268
6. Grimsby, before 1240
7. Scarborough, before 1240

Custody of Newcastle

1. Newcastle, before 1239
2. Richmond, 1257-8 (?)
3. Hartlepool, before 1240
4. Carlisle, 1233
5. Berwick, 1231 (?) (before 1281)[1]
6. Roxburgh, before 1235
7. Haddington, before 1242
8. Dundee, before 1296
9. Dumfries, before 1264

Short-lived Foundations

Romney (Kent), 1241
Durham, 1239

Later Foundations

Walsingham, 1347
Ware, before 1351[2]
Plymouth, 1383
Aylesbury, 1387

APPENDIX II

Rhyming Ten Commandments

"Take no God but on in hewene,
Name nowth his name in gy disstewene,
Loke ryth iwel thin halyday,
Thin fader and moder thu worchepe hav,
Loke thow be no man sleer,
Ne fals wytnesse thow ne beer,
Thow schalt don non lecherye,
Ne non thefte of felonye,
Thin neyzebour godus thu ne swille,
Nee wyf ne dowtyr for to spille,
These ben the hastes of gret mede,
Wyt hem wel and thu schalt spede."

This version, taken from Friar Staunton's *De decem preceptis,* was published by G. R. Owst in the *Dublin Review,* 1925, pp. 278 *et seq.* Friar Staunton was an English Franciscan who flourished as a preacher probably in the early fourteenth century (Owst, *loc. cit.*). As this or similar versions of rhyming Ten Commandments occurred in various Mss. of the period, the real authorship is not determined. Dr. Little publishes a slightly different version from the *Fasciculus morum* in his *Studies in English Franciscan History,* p. 150.

---

1. 1244? See Bryce, *Scottish Grey Friars.*
2. 1338-9? See license to acquire land and build, Feb. 18, 1338 (*Cal. Pat., 1338-1340,* p. 14).

APPENDIX III

Brother Bozon's Preaching of Bad and Unfair Lords

"The vulture is very cruel toward his fledglings, as the philosopher Pliny says, for so soon as he perceives that fat grows on their body he beats them with his wings, and pecks them with his beak, until they become thin. Then he loves them and acclaims them as his own. So do they if they use the beak to slander and threaten, and beat the wings of mastery and will, until their fledglings — that is to say, their tenants — can gain no fatness. Wherefore says our Lord through Jeremy, 'Also in thy wings is found the blood of the souls of the poor innocents' (Jer. ii, 34). Through the two wings of riches — mastery and will — are the poor put under foot. It goes on, 'Yet thou sayest, Because I am innocent' (35)."

This is "J. R's" translation of Parable 6. Evidently it is but the theme or skeleton of a longer sermon, but it illustrates Brother Bozon's method.

Modern friars who knot their girdles and people who tie strings around their fingers as an aid to memory will be interested in the following evidence that the ideas are not new. Speaking on the theme that Christ will not forget us sinners, Brother Bozon has this to say:

"Jesus Christ, our sweet Friend, Son of the King of heaven, Who, through pure love and pity that He had for us wretched prisoners, came to visit and comfort us in this prison, and then, on His return, to remember us in the heavenly court, has us so dear that He will not knot His girdle nor wear a ring on His finger in remembrance, but from wounds that He suffered for us He will see a sign remaining in Him that we are very dear to Him in heart — that His goodness may be very dear to us" (from "J. R.'s" translation of Parable 79).

APPENDIX IV

I Will Become A Friar

"No more ne willi wiked be,
Forsake ich wille this world-is fe,
this wildis wedis this folen gle;
ich wul be mild of chere,
of cnottis scal me girdil be,
becomen ich wil frere.

"Frere menur i wil me make,
and lecherie i wille asake;
to ihesu christ ich wil me take
and serue in holi churche,
al in mi ouris for to wake,
goddis wille to wurche.

"Wurche i wille this workes gode,
for him that boyht us in the rode;
from his side ran the blode,
so dere he gon us bie —
for sothe i tel him more than wode
that hautit licherie."

From Carleton Brown, ed., *English Lyrics of the Thirteenth Century* (Oxford, 1932), p. 126. I have modernized the "th" sign.

INDEX

CORRECTIONS AND ADDITIONS

P. 7, l. 7: for "May 3" read "September 10"; footnote 15: delete "Eccleston . . . arrival."

P. 9, footnote 26: for "81" read "28."

P. 17, footnote 60: add "et seq."

P. 22, footnote 87: delete "Dugdale . . . 1545."

P. 36, footnote 50: insert "p." before "36."

P. 37, footnote 53: read "Die Fruehesten," etc.

P. 43, footnote 87: for "627" read "626 and 627."

P. 49, footnote 8: for "chap. iv" read "chap. vi."

P. 50, footnote 13: tr. "C. L. Kingsford" after "London."

P. 52, footnote 29: for "Close Rolls" read "Cal. Close."

P. 61, footnote 89: for "166-68" read "141 et seq."; footnote 90: for "II, 318" read "I, 318."

P. 83, footnote 89: for "Regesta" read "Regestra."

P. 85, footnote 102: for "this page" read "p. 88."

P. 88, footnote 126: for "H. R." read "H. G."

P. 89, l. 2: read "order at Assisi."

P. 91, l. 22: for "1207" read "1307"; footnote 145: for "533" read "553."

P. 94, l. 8: for "he also thought" read "he also thinks."

P. 108, l. 25: read "Midelton Abbey."

P. 112, l. 26: read "Albert of Pisa"; footnote 69: read "Little's Eccleston."

P. 121, l. 11: for "they begin" read "the friars begin."